KV-213-462

THE MILLENNIUM MANAGER

THE
CHANGE
MASTER

Managing and
Adapting to
Organisational Change

MITCH McCRIMMON

the Institute
of Management

FOUNDATION

PITMAN
PUBLISHING

London · Hong Kong · Johannesburg
Melbourne · Singapore · Washington DC

The Sheffield College

Hillsborough LRC
☎ 0114 2602254

Acc. No.
111458465

WITHDRAWN

Class
658.8

Loan Category
ORD

PITMAN PUBLISHING
128 Long Acre, London WC2E 9AN
Tel: +44 (0)171 447 2000
Fax: +44(0)171 240 5771

A Division of Pearson Professional Limited

First published in Great Britain in 1997

© Pearson Professional Limited 1997

The right of Mitch McCrimmon to be identified as author
of this work has been asserted by him in accordance
with the Copyright, Designs and Patents Act 1988.

ISBN 0 273 62632 9

British Library Cataloguing in Publication Data
A CIP catalogue record for this book can be obtained from the British Library

All rights reserved; no part of this publication may be reproduced, stored
in a retrieval system, or transmitted in any form or by any means, electronic,
mechanical, photocopying, recording, or otherwise without either the prior
written permission of the Publishers or a licence permitting restricted copying
in the United Kingdom issued by the Copyright Licensing Agency Ltd,
90 Tottenham Court Road, London W1P 9HE. This book may not be lent,
resold, hired out or otherwise disposed of by way of trade in any form
of binding or cover other than that in which it is published, without the
prior consent of the Publishers.

10 9 8 7 6 5 4 3 2 1

Typeset by PanTek Arts, Maidstone, Kent
Printed and bound in Great Britain by Bell and Bain Ltd, Glasgow

The Publishers' policy is to use paper manufactured from sustainable forests.

THE
CHANGE MASTER

THE SHEFFIELD COLLEGE

111458465

Sheffield

The Institute of Management (IM) is at the forefront of management development and best management practice. The Institute embraces all levels of management from students to chief executives. It provides a unique portfolio of services for all managers, enabling them to develop skills and achieve management excellence.

If you would like to hear more about the benefits of membership, please write to Department P, Institute of Management, Cottingham Road, Corby NN17 1TT.

This series is commissioned by the Institute of Management Foundation.

ABOUT THE AUTHOR

Mitch McCrimmon, PhD, is a Chartered Psychologist with the British Psycological Society. He has worked in consulting and human resources management for 22 years, initially in Canada and for 10 years now in the United Kingdom. His firm, the Self Renewal Group, focuses on the development of senior managers. An earlier book, *Unleash the Entrepreneur Within* (1995), also published by Pitman, dealt with how large organisations can be more entrepreneurial. Other writings can be found in a regular column for *Human Resources* magazine. His web site for managers, *Managing yourself, leading others*, at www.srg.co.uk, offers practical suggestions on a wide range of topics pertaining to executive self-renewal.

CONTENTS

PART 2 • CONFRONTING THE HARD TRANSITIONS

FOREWORD

The Institute of Management's study *Management Development to the Millennium* confirmed that the demands on managers today are very different from those of ten, or even five, years ago. The demands of the new century will be even more different.

However managers should welcome the pressures that today's dynamic marketplace puts upon them – managing change to achieve something better is a principal, probably on-going task of management.

As the management world has become very much more complicated, a key skill is to be prepared for, and wherever possible predict, the changes that will occur in future. New technology, changing markets and changing organisational cultures are all crucially important influences on managers' behaviour and activities.

Technology is the key to combining the advantages of a very large organisation with the advantages of a very small one, while the competitive nature of the national and global marketplace means that total quality is becoming the minimum standard required to compete. Cultural changes however can never be forced. In a learning organisation there has to be a shift from dominant attention to short-term success towards creating a context that stimulates managers to experiment with opportunities in favour of long-term growth. Organisations must be dynamic – they have to change, both out of necessity and by choice. The manager's job of today therefore focuses more on action and less on analysis, with more emphasis on intervention than on planning. These changes are happening in almost all organisations, both large and small, in both the private and public sectors. So whether you work for a giant multinational or a small local company, it is likely that you will have to change your way of working to keep up with the shifts in your market and benefit from the new opportunities of the new century.

I therefore unreservedly commend *The Millennium Manager* series both for its forward-looking approach and for continuing the debate around the direction of management and management development for UK plc.

Roger Young
Director General, Institute of Management

Hillsborough College
Learning Resource Centre
Telephone 0114 2602254

PRIORITY SKILLS FOR THE MANAGER OF 2001

In July 1995, the Institute of Management published a report, *Management Development to the Millennium*, based on interviews with opinion formers at the most senior managerial level of industry and commerce – all who had high expectations of their managers in their ability to lead and grow their organisations.

Managers are expected to have the ability to operate across a broad range of skills and competencies. The *Management Development to the Millennium* report identified those skills and competencies that senior managers felt were essential for management and organisational success into the new millennium.

The following table from the report shows a list of the priority skills selected by respondents. Three-quarters of the managers surveyed indicated a clear focus on the 'harder' skills of strategic thinking and change management. Nevertheless, over four in ten endorsed the importance of facilitating others to contribute, in other words a classic 'softer' skill.

Skills for the manager in the next millennium

Base: 1,241 respondents	%
Strategic thinking, eg longer term, broader perspective, anticipating	78
✓ Responding to and managing change	75
An orientation towards total quality/customer satisfaction	67
Financial management, eg role and impact of key financial indicators	46
Facilitating others to contribute	44
Understanding the role of information and IT	42
Verbal communication, eg coherent, persuasive	38
Organisational sensitivity, eg cross-functional understanding	37
Risk assessment in decision making	35

This book addresses the indicated skill – *responding to and managing change*. Other books in the **Pitman/IM Millennium Manager** series concentrate on some of the other skills listed above.

FACING THE MONSTER

Are you ready:

- for the pace of change to double?
- to face the demand for even more efficiency?
- to be much more innovative?
- to keep obsolescence at bay as it races ever faster to overtake you?
- to manage with much less power than you have today?
- to face more frequent and more extensive changes?
- to let go of more control despite the pressure for more accountability?
- to face even more uncertainty and ambiguity?
- to move ahead without knowing where you are going?
- to admit that you have very few of the answers?

This is a book on the psychology of change. It is intended to help managers understand and cope with personal efforts to change more successfully.

Simple change formulas do not work. More communication and extra hype can actually increase the fear of change. Glorifying the virtues of being thin to a fat person just increases his anxiety, driving him to eat more rather than diet. Why should organisational change be any easier?

Resistance to change is too deep-seated to overcome without directly confronting our underlying fears. As the pace of change accelerates, the need for a deeper understanding of change becomes urgent.

This book is not directly about managing large-scale organisational change. It is about how individuals personally react to change and how they can be more effective in adapting and preparing for it.

Reading this book will help managers to:

- better understand why they and their employees resist change
- cope more effectively with change and initiate it more confidently
- help others overcome their resistance to change
- prepare for specific types of role change, and
- prepare to deal effectively with even more change in the future.

PREPARING FOR THE 21ST CENTURY

As we approach the new millennium, the pace of change is escalating geometrically. The way you work is changing faster than ever. Your business is in continuous upheaval and the world is rapidly shrinking. Instant news from around the globe only makes us more aware of how many people we are competing against. It is as if we are at war – with instant communications only making us see how much closer the enemy is than we thought.

All of the fears and anxieties we feel in relation to change will be brought into the open in this book. This is the only way to begin developing some strategies for managing change rather than being driven by it.

At worst, we think of change as a monster that will confront us suddenly and devour us. We feel this generalised dread that the monster of change will creep into our office any day now and declare us obsolete, of no use to anybody. As the pace of change increases, the more we feel vulnerable and the closer the monster seems. We view change as a monster partly because we

tend to think in global terms, i.e. everything is great, lousy, black, white, etc. Global thinking applied to our fears makes matters worse because we can do less about something global than we can about something specific. Doing nothing increases anxiety as we then feel less in control, more at the mercy of whatever we are afraid of.

Adult fears are not much different from childhood fears. Like children, in a state of fear, we all too readily hope someone will save us. But as adults we fear that no one is there to protect us, so we are overtaken by a greater sense of being alone. Feeling alone, of course, only adds to our anxiety. Many of us feel too embarrassed to talk about such fears, partly because everyone around us seems to be getting on with things well enough, making us think that we must be the only ones feeling afraid. And how embarrassing it would be to admit to fears that no one else feels.

FACING OUR FEARS AND ANXIETIES

We need to understand our anxieties and the reasons behind them in order to manage them effectively. We also need to get a handle on how to think differently about change and about our roles. Most importantly, we need an action plan: it is really only through activity that we can minimise anxiety. Not just random activity, but highly focused activity. We must regain a sense of achieving something worthwhile and of being in control of our own destiny if we are to manage change comfortably and turn it to our own advantage. Tangible achievement and a sense of mastery contribute more to greater self-confidence and anxiety reduction than any amount of introspection or soul searching alone could ever do.

No fear of change?

Not afraid of the change monster you say? No doubt some of us are too anxious about too many things. Others have a convenient way of blocking out even the slightest concern. The former are too paralysed by fear to improve their receptiveness to change while the latter are determined to wait until it hits them before allowing themselves to think about it. Neither is able to prepare for change, hence both are about as adaptable as the dinosaur. Shutting out fear and anxiety can of course be a form of healthy self-protection, not unlike our immune system, but too much obliviousness to danger is the best way to be hardest hit by it.

Perhaps you have enjoyed all the changes you have lived through thus far. But change, for all of us, is whatever alters the way *we* think our world should work. So maybe you just haven't come across this sort of change yet. Nothing has yet disturbed your picture of how things should work. Does this mean you are prepared to adapt to a picture that conflicts with yours? Probably not. Hence the possible benefits of reading this book.

Even large organisations are now learning that there is no failure like success – meaning that constant success (thus far) is poor preparation for inevitable change.

A basic fact of life regarding change

➲ **No one can keep up with change at today's pace, never mind tomorrow's.**

Change occurs faster than we can keep up with it partly because of technology but mainly because younger people, or those new to our industry, keep leapfrogging us into the future. So this is not a book about how to be superhuman. The issue is about how to manage as much change as we can handle, constructively, and to learn to live with falling behind.

TOMORROW'S CHANGE AGENDA

Let's take a closer at some of the changes that managers are increasingly having to face.

1. More efficiency, more innovation

How can you squeeze more productivity out of overstretched resources? Surely only by working smarter, by thinking creatively about how to do more with less. The same applies to product or service innovation: more creativity is the essential ingredient. This is a major personal change issue because of our perverse tendency to become comfortable with the familiar. It is hard enough adapting to major change let alone thinking creatively about how to initiate it ourselves. But no one doubts that increasingly intense competition will force us to search constantly for productivity improvements and to develop innovative new offerings.

➲ **The difficulty is that, exceptions to the contrary, most of us tend to become *consolidators* rather than *innovators* as we age.**

2. Petrifying obsolescence

In the dawning age of the knowledge worker, keeping up-to-date is itself becoming a full-time job. Worse, it's too big a job for any one person, even within specialised fields. In the good old days, managers could gracefully grow away from their specialised knowledge base and become 'general managers' – mere co-ordinators. Now, power is shifting to knowledge, away from position, hence the unrelenting pressure to keep up with the content of some specialised knowledge base (assuming you want to retain some influence).

The idea of becoming a content-free general manager was never more than a myth anyway. So-called general managers have always kept a grasp on their credibility and power by virtue of what they know, their ability to decide which direction to pursue, not because of their skills as co-ordinators. The liability of any general management role has just become more obvious today as the difficulty of knowing enough about a whole business becomes ever-more conspicuous. If its nigh on impossible to keep up with more than a highly specialised field today, how do you know what knowledge will be relevant tomorrow? Again, the issue is not so much about learning faster as one of continually finding new ways of adding value while simultaneously maintaining a hold on your sanity.

3. Preserving a semblance of control with less power

➲ Democracy = more choice for all = less power for any one person.

The business world is fast going democratic. It is not only consumers who are spoiled for choice. As a business entity, your organisation has more stakeholders who have more influence than ever before. These include shareholders, suppliers, joint venture partners, the government, even your competitors. Employees have more power as well – not in the old-fashioned unionised sense but by virtue of their growing knowledge and the greater dependency you have on them for your success. Empowerment is not just about managers buying the benefits of delegation it is also about waking up to the fact that knowledge now held by employees gives them more power whether managers like it or not. The so-called information age will only speed up the democratisation of business.

Today's managers are like royalty, being forced to adjust to a world in which they have less power. In the most developed knowledge industries, such as the legal and medical professions, it is the professionals who have all the power. The managers occupy more of a service role. How will managers adjust to this change? To what extent do they even see it coming? What shape will their future roles take? How will they add value in a knowledge driven industry?

4. Major personal role changes

Mobility from one employer to another will increase. Industries that most depend on doing something completely different – fast – will benefit from more cross-fertilization. Moving to a bigger job in a different organisation has never been especially easy. Today's rate of change will mean that you will have less time to prove your worth, while your successes, as well as your failures, will be more visible. The demand to add value quickly will be a tall order in businesses of growing complexity. Scepticism on the part of insiders will put added pressure on your adaptability skills.

Businesses will continue to spin off subsidiaries and acquire others, requiring you to step in, perhaps at short notice and produce amazing results quickly. So, you can expect faster changes to new roles, more sudden increases in responsibility and more demands to take on roles for which you may be completely unprepared.

Taking all these changes together we have a recipe for greater anxiety and resistance to change, especially if you are experiencing them all at the same time!

5. Letting go

➲ **It is pretty hard to move somewhere else without leaving where you are now.**

Hanging onto the past is seemingly a favourite pastime judging from its pervasiveness. Managers hang onto remnants of old roles. Under pressure, we are most comfortable doing what we do best and this is often something we should be delegating. Making a success of change is not possible without making a success of letting go. Faster change will mean more anxiety generally and this will make letting go harder. Anxiety is only reduced through some form of comfort, usually gained from the familiar.

Managers are failing to let go when they get angry at a younger subordinate for knowing something they do not know, or when, after a promotion, they still want to do their old jobs as well as their new ones. They often need to keep busy with their old jobs to gain continual reassurance that they know what to do and, through being too busy, creating a ready excuse if they fail in their new jobs.

As mandatory retirement disappears, the dreaded final departure needs to be seen as just one more career change, but only the skilled at letting go will manage it gracefully. Letting go is hardest at this stage and a better understanding of why this is so will shed light on the dynamics of letting go generally.

PLAN OF THIS BOOK

Part 1

This part deals with the manifold ways in which managers resist change. It deals with the fear and resentment of change and how we can overcome our anxieties to face the future more confidently. A major theme of this part is that we need to be more entrepreneurial in the face of change and less reactive or defensive. We also examine the relationship between low self-esteem and fear of change in this part of the book. Practical steps are outlined to help make this way of dealing with the unwelcome as realistic as possible for you. In addition, we look at the personal traits or skills you should consider cultivating in yourself in order to be as effective at adjusting to change as you would like to be.

Part 2

This part applies what we have learned in Part 1 to some of the most challenging changes managers will have to face as we round the corner of the new millennium. We begin by looking at one of the most poorly handled personal transitions of them all. This is the transition to a bigger job in a different organisation. You all know the meaning of the 'new broom' jargon, that an incoming boss tends to 'sweep aside' inherited subordinates. While some of this bloodshed is no doubt justified, it will be argued here that a great deal of it amounts to a poor ability to cope with personal transitions. The inability to adjust to such a major role change applies to both the incoming executive and his inherited subordinates. We will then use the analysis of this role change to shed light on other role changes.

In this part we will also look at the need to let go of old roles and preconceptions by looking at situations where managers often hang on so rigidly, that they end up making fools of themselves. Looking closely at what is going on here will help us to see ways in which we fail to let go effectively in other contexts and what we can do about it. Finally, we close with some comments on facing change as the new millennium approaches.

➲ **If you are keen to confront the big transitions head on and without delay, you can read Part 2 of this book ahead of Part 1.**

'Change is not made without inconvenience,
even from worse to better.'

Samuel Johnson, *Dictionary*

PART 1

TAMING THE EMOTIONAL ROLLER-COASTER

'Our doubts are traitors.
And make us lose the good we oft might win
By fearing to attempt.'

Shakespeare, *Measure for Measure*

CHAPTER

EVERYONE'S RESISTANCE TO CHANGE

OBJECTIVE

- To gain an understanding of resistance to change by looking at why some managers fear or resent change and how their reactions to change are affected by their levels of self-esteem.

INTRODUCTION

Everyone does *not* resist change, you say. You thrive on it. Its somebody else's problem. The only issue for you is why everyone else is so inflexible.

But resistance to change has become the business world's number one disease, so debilitating is it in blocking desperately needed organisational improvements. Because of the severity of the affliction, consultants have bombarded us with quick fix prescriptions to help us change faster. Yet resistance seems to be growing or at least not yielding. Without doubt, managers who can best cope with change personally and help others to do likewise will be much in demand as we approach the millennium.

In this chapter, we will attempt to clarify what change is and why some people seem to resist it more than others, making a start at getting to grips with two of the more common causes of resistance to change:

- fear, and
- resentment.

FEAR OF CHANGE

We will look at the problem of entrenched habits later. Fear and resentment are psychological reactions to unwelcome events, while entrenched habits are sustained partly by the immediate environment and partly by the sort of person you are. An example of struggling to break an unwanted habit would be trying to diet when your friends and family eat all they want in front of you. Your struggle is made difficult by your own needs plus being in an environment that is not highly conducive to dieting.

Further, those who resist change because of entrenched habits often accept the need to change in principle – they may even be change champions for a while. It is just that they keep slipping back into old ways – like trying frequently to quit smoking but continuing to fail. Those who fear or resent change, on the other

5

hand, do not want to change. They would prefer to preserve the status quo.

Getting to grips with the fear and resentment of change

Looking first at resistance based on fear and resentment, we need to understand how these feelings keep managers from changing and who is most likely to be affected by them. Whether you are interested in being a change champion in the next century or just getting through the day, perhaps you might like to take stock of your current feelings about change.

Your attitude to change

To do a quick audit of your attitudes to change, answer true or false to each of the questions in the *change attitude audit* (see Figure 1.1). Doing this change attitude audit for yourself is not a matter of getting the right answers or a particular score, it is about

---

CHANGE ATTITUDE AUDIT

		True	False
1.	I anticipate change with a feeling of dread.	☐	☐
2.	I would be bored without regular change.	☐	☐
3.	I am oblivious to change. It doesn't affect me at all.	☐	☐
4.	I have experienced major change and it was awful.	☐	☐
5.	Change is O.K. so long as it comes in small doses.	☐	☐
6.	The only changes I like are the ones I initiate.	☐	☐
7.	We seem to change just for the sake of it.	☐	☐
8.	Too many people are too slow to accept change.	☐	☐
9.	Change is often more damaging than beneficial.	☐	☐
10.	Change resisters must be pushed on or pushed out.	☐	☐

Fig 1.1

being as honest with yourself as you can be. Try to really think about the meaning of change when you answer the questions.

➲ **The point of this audit is to ask you to think hard about what change really means beyond the simple formulae and hype.**

Have you really experienced major change?

Some people think they enjoy change. But change is in the eye of the beholder. What might be disruptive change for you could be a favourite pastime for me. How is it that the same event is not even noticed by one person and, at the same time, is a major trauma for someone else? The answer must be that change really is in the eye of the beholder.

You may enjoy what is a major change for someone else, but it is not really change for you unless some fundamental aspect of your identity is threatened. If you are a new technology freak, introducing more of it may be a change for others but it is your bread and butter. Having to live without technology would be a change for you.

It is just as important to understand why some people seem to relish change as it is to understand why others cannot cope with it. If you find change difficult, it won't be made easier for you to see others enjoying it. You will only feel worse about yourself and want even greater reassurance and stronger sources of security.

Getting clear about why some people sail through change will help us learn how to handle it more easily ourselves. It is some comfort to know that many of our colleagues only apparently enjoy change. It is not that they are necessarily better at dealing with change; it is rather that they have no *personal stake* in the way things are. A major change for us is no big deal for them. Still other people neither fear nor especially enjoy change – until it hits them where it hurts. Then it is the worst disaster of their lives.

Those of you who feel you relish change may genuinely enjoy doing new and different things. But for most people, 'new and different' falls within a pretty narrow band of all the possible things in the world they could try. Hence most people who say they enjoy change may never really have experienced it – not, at least, in the sense of their self-esteem or identity being under threat. Many managers you discuss change with face to face, claim they don't mind change, so it is something of a mystery who is doing all the resisting. The suspicion cannot be avoided that some managers are less adaptable than they think they are or like to make out.

While you may not be bothered by the changes exercising everyone else in your organisation at the moment, you really may not be well-prepared to cope with personally threatening change. So, even if you don't see a need to improve your ability to cope with current changes, you may want to prepare yourself for the future.

➲ **Change will come faster and it gets harder as we get older.**

Without doubt, most of us will either fear or resent some changes at some time in our careers, so any effort we make now to improve our ability to deal with change will be worthwhile. Those of us who are most strongly aware of our fear of change tend to imagine change as a sort of monster about to enter our office at any time and devour us.

Either we fear the monster or we are good at thinking that disasters always happen to somebody else. The defensive approach may get you through today, but leave you ill-prepared if the monster suddenly comes for you. The unknown is fearful in direct proportion to how safe you feel with the known. The downside of feeling too comfortable with the known is that you may be too dependent on it. Clearly the more you depend on the known the harder it will be for you to face the unknown. Excessive reliance on the familiar tends to go hand in hand with low self-esteem. It is likely that those with low self-esteem feel the most fear of change.

> *The suspicion cannot be avoided that some managers are less adaptable than they think they are or like to make out.*

People with a high level of self-esteem tend to *resent* change rather than fear it. Their resistance can be very active and aggressive while the fearful simply await their fate, hoping to avoid it rather than take charge of events.

At this point, you may be thinking that this is all exaggeration, that you have never felt any fear of change in your life. Unfortunately, many people only experience fear of change when it is too late – after they have been made redundant, for example, and then begun to realise how dependent they were on the job they lost and the people they worked with for so many years. Or you're in the middle of a major organisational change and you have been dragging your feet – until your boss starts to lay down the law and you finally feel threatened.

One reason we may not feel as much fear of change as we might is that we are highly skilled at avoiding the unpleasant. We excel at pretending that everything is fine and will go on smoothly forever.

We generally blame others or external circumstances first and ourselves only as a last resort.

Self-deception, however inadvertent it may be, is like a drug that prevents us from seeing danger until reality hits us in the face and knocks us off our feet.

Fear of change can take different forms. You may not be lying awake at night shaking with fear, but you may be excessively driving yourself to keep up-to-date or to retain control of some aspect of your job. Or you may feel irritable with everyone for no obvious reason. Perhaps you feel very angry that your superiors have got everything wrong at the moment. We generally blame others or external circumstances first and ourselves only as a last resort. Not consciously feeling fear doesn't mean you aren't propelled by it.

EXAMPLES

Take my friend Tony, a 45-year-old engineering manager with a large consumer electronics manufacturer. He won't admit, even to himself, that he is afraid of obsolescence, but he drives himself harder than anyone I know to keep up-to-date with his field. And he can get very angry if one of his younger subordinates appears to know something he doesn't. Tony can't decide whether to retain his identity as a technical guru or focus on being a manager, so he struggles to do both and ends up doing neither very well.

And what about Bert. At 50, he is still regarded as the hero who introduced the first computers into his company nearly 30 years ago. But now a wholly new use of information technology has been introduced and Bert was made redundant because he dragged his feet for two years during the implementation of the new system. Bert was seen as a radical champion of change in his early days. Why is he so resistant to change now?

Perhaps Bert is just over the hill you say. But then there is Heather who at 26 was the youngest marketing director ever appointed at a large food processing company. She championed the introduction of several new product groups but couldn't accept the new Chief Executive's decision to take a different direction, so at 28 she resigned.

A major insurance company was implementing a large-scale empowerment initiative, but had to fire their Finance Director because he simply could not let go of day-to-day details. He used his functional hat as an excuse to over-control his department because he was afraid of losing his job if he let go of so much responsibility. So he lost it anyway.

What do all of these managers have in common? I said above that change is 'not change for you unless some fundamental aspect of your identity is threatened'. In each of these examples, the managers involved were faced with some sort of identity crisis. Tony could not decide whether to identify with the role of technical expert or manager. Bert identified too closely with a particular computer system because he was seen as a hero for implementing it. Heather was so publicly associated with the new range of products she introduced, that it was too much of a loss of face for her to accept having to discontinue them after only two years on the market.

But these are high-profile people with a lot of public personal investment in something. Why then do employees in less visible jobs resist change?

A colleague of mine could not understand why her 25-year-old secretary, Sally, should be so wedded to the company's manual filing system. Surely it is not that important. But Sally had low self-esteem for a number of reasons. She had the least education of all the secretaries in her department and she had just broken up with her boyfriend. With the least seniority among the secretaries, Sally felt she had to make herself indispensable. The familiar routines of her job were all she had to give her a sense of security, of being in control of, and good at, something. So she needed these routines, but more importantly, being told to adopt a new filing system felt, at the time, like being told she could not do anything right. She had to hang onto something to avoid feeling worthless. Even though Sally is not in a high-profile role in the company, she had no other immediate source of self-esteem and pride so she could not give it up without a battle.

WHAT IS CHANGE ANYWAY?

Every second the world changes in a multitude of ways, though we hardly notice more than a few of them. Changing your clothes to go out for the evening is usually just as unremarkable. We know that moving house, being fired, changing jobs voluntarily or getting divorced are major traumas for most people, especially if they are first time events. If change is in the eye of the beholder, then real change for you is only that which completely throws you off course and causes you to wonder who you are or where you are going. It is this type of change that most of us are poorly prepared for. Because we have never experienced it, we don't naturally know how to prepare for it. It is easy enough to prepare for a hurricane after you have survived the first one.

If you doubt that change is in the eye of the beholder, just consider how differently people react to the same event. Having to move the desks in the office around slightly can seem momentously trivial to some employees while it can be upsetting to others. How change affects us depends on two ingredients:

● how different the situation is from what it was, and
● how much we have invested in the old ways.

11

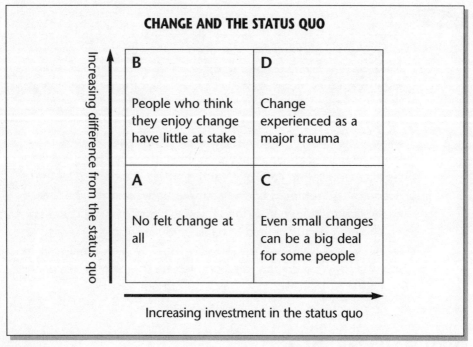

CHANGE AND THE STATUS QUO

Increasing difference from the status quo →

B	D
People who think they enjoy change have little at stake	Change experienced as a major trauma
A	C
No felt change at all	Even small changes can be a big deal for some people

Increasing investment in the status quo →

Fig 1.2

Our *investment* in the status quo is greatest if we are highly dependent on it for our self-esteem and identity – our basic conception of who we are and what our purpose is.

As you can see in Figure 1.2, *Box A* represents minimal external change in the status quo. But you are completely indifferent to how things are done in this context anyway because you have nothing at stake here. *Box B* is where we find people who say they relish change when, for them, it is not really change at all because they feel no dependency on the status quo. These people seem to enjoy change, even quite large-scale changes, but the reality is that they have no stake in the older ways, so it does not really feel like major change to them.

We find my colleague's secretary, Sally, in *Box C* because she had a lot of pride and self-esteem invested in what, to others, were quite inconsequential procedures. I don't mean to suggest that only clerical employees are in this box. A senior executive might have a lot at stake in the wording of his title – something that would be trivial to others.

Change really becomes a problem, however, for anyone in *Box D*. The difference between *then* and *now* is huge and the Box D people define their whole existence in terms of *then*. People in Box D won't feel any greater trauma than those in Box C, but major organisational changes fall into Box D and they are the ones that primarily interest us. Box C is also important though because it is so easy for change agents to overlook people in this box. It seems so unreasonable for such people to resist change that we naturally take no steps to ease them through it. Resistance in Box C, when changes are apparently trivial, probably cause the most anger on the part of the promoters of change because resistance here seems so irrational to them.

The key point of all of this is that the scale of change is not really the most critical factor. What really matters is the degree to which you depend on a given state of affairs for your identity and purpose in life.

So, regardless of the scale of the changes your organisation is going through – large or small – it is essential to consider how much employees might have invested in keeping things the way they are.

Self-esteem, identity and resistance to change

The underlying theme here is that, for different reasons, we all depend on some activity or occupation for our self-esteem and identity. It is through *doing* things rather than *being* a certain type of person that we get feedback and any sense of accomplishment. And it is mainly through accomplishing tasks that we learn, or decide, who we are. We identify with an occupation to the extent that we have no equally important source of self-esteem, or to the extent that we feel a high degree of pride in having independently achieved something.

Highly-sociable employees will identify closely with a group, so acceptance rather than rejection will be critically important for them. Conversely, you might have a high-profile role where you have committed yourself publicly to a course of action but still not identify so totally with it that you cannot give it up. On the other hand, your occupation can be quite low-profile, but you may need to feel in control of it because it is your only source of self-esteem.

WHAT IS FEAR OF CHANGE?

Fear of change is the fear of being out of control, of being seen as, or feeling, useless. We fear loss of everything we have worked to achieve: a sense of being on top of things and of being well-regarded by others. On a deeper level we tend to see our lives as a journey or a race. Fear of change is like being in a race and being told we missed a turning a long way back and now have to start all over again. Life is like a race in the sense that we feel we have limited time to get wherever we are going. Having to start all over again is not just a loss of time it is like being demoted: you feel that now you will have to be a peer to people who were once your juniors and this is total loss of face. If you are afraid of change, you will go out of your way to avoid it. This may even be how you display your greatest creativity at work!

> *Fear of change is like being in a race and being told we missed a turning a long way back and now have to start all over again.*

The pace of change

Our fear of losing control is not just a function of the magnitude of a change or of how much we have invested in the old way of doing things. Another very important variable is the sheer *pace* of change confronting so many organisations today. For a lot of managers, there is little time to get hooked on any status quo because none lasts long enough. Such people have gone past the stage of fearing loss of control and are just helplessly drifting. They are in a permanent state of cynicism or burnout and they feel they can do nothing about it. They may also feel an unhealthy degree of dependence on their leaders – hoping that their leaders will somehow carry them through.

In Figure 1.3, you can see that, as the fear of loss of control grows, *Box B*, employees can become increasingly fearful of even gradual or small changes.

Employees in *Box C* either don't mind being out of control or they have a sense of control over enough aspects of their lives that they do not mind the ambiguity that often accompanies some organisational changes. Or they feel so confident generally, that no crisis or even failure can dent their high self-esteem, so they know that they have nothing to fear, no matter what happens.

Box D, again, represents the worst scenario because fear of losing control is highest and so is the pace of change. The result is a feeling of panic at first, followed by a state of resignation and hopelessness. If you notice yourself or colleagues displaying a lot of cynicism or sarcasm, chances are they have slipped into the resignation stage.

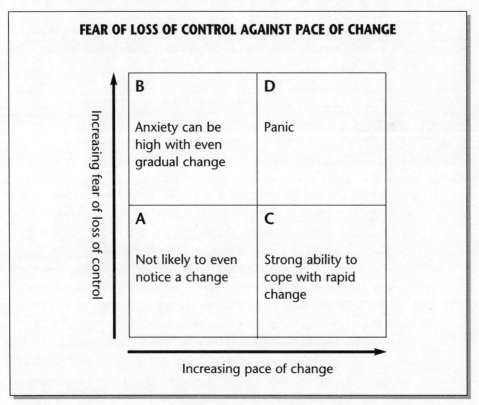

FEAR OF LOSS OF CONTROL AGAINST PACE OF CHANGE

B	D
Anxiety can be high with even gradual change	Panic
A	C
Not likely to even notice a change	Strong ability to cope with rapid change

Increasing fear of loss of control

Increasing pace of change

Fig 1.3

When resistance is greatest

Combining the two boxes in Figures 1.1 and 1.2, it becomes evident that resistance to change based on fear or resentment will be greatest when:

- major organisational change occurs
- employees have a lot personally invested in the status quo
- change is imposed
- the pace of change is high, and
- employees have a strong fear of losing control.

It is not simply that some employees start with a tendency to invest a lot in their work or to have a strong need to be in control, although some people do have these personality traits. More importantly, it is the sheer pace and magnitude of change itself that often cause employees to want to grab onto something solid in the first place, so it is a bit of a vicious circle.

➪ It is because the pace of change is anxiety producing in itself that it adds to any anxiety managers feel about change for other reasons.

RESENTMENT OF CHANGE

Fear of change or resentment?

In the midst of change, you may be feeling resentment rather than fear. We only fear what we think might hurt us in some way. Fear is also a function of self-esteem. If you have high self-esteem, you are confident that, no matter what happens, you will get through it somehow. You feel that your personal resources are resilient enough to *control* most of what will happen to you so that you can adjust to any eventuality. Those who lack this degree of self-esteem tend to feel more at the mercy of events or the whim of the powerful – in other words, less in control of their fate. This is an important distinction because we will have to approach our own resistance to change and that of others quite differently depending on whether resistance is based on fear or resentment.

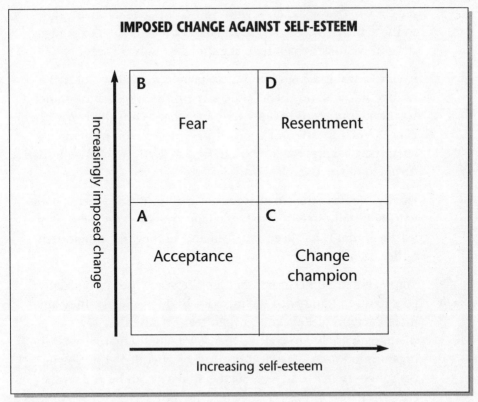

IMPOSED CHANGE AGAINST SELF-ESTEEM

Increasingly imposed change →

B Fear	**D** Resentment
A Acceptance	**C** Change champion

Increasing self-esteem →

Fig 1.4

As you can see in Figure 1.4, those in *Box A*, have low self-esteem, but change is not imposed. They feel involved and valued, so they accept the change. However, their self-confidence is too low to enable them be real leaders of change. Acceptance is the best you can hope for in this case.

Moving to *Box B*, we find those who experience the most fear because change is highly imposed and they have low self-esteem. These people feel fear because they see themselves as having no control over anything, so they feel most vulnerable, most at the mercy of their fate. The unknown is scary because they are the most unsure whether they will be able to cope with it. Even if they feel no fear in advance of the changes being implemented, their fear may get in the way as they begin to see how the changes affect them. (I am assuming here that we are dealing with people who also have a high stake in the status quo.) Most people with low self-esteem will overly attach themselves to one state of affairs, however, so those with low self-esteem will almost inevitably have a high stake in whatever gives them the strongest sense of security.

In *Box C*, we find high self-esteem people who have not had change imposed on them. Their sense of their own importance has been confirmed because they have been consulted. Win them over by such means and you will have gained some change champions – employees who can help to lead the change initiative throughout the organisation.

Finally, we have the worst scenario again in *Box D* where people with high self-esteem have had change imposed on them or at least feel that it has been imposed and so they feel resentment rather than fear

Employees in Box D are often high fliers as self-esteem usually goes hand in hand with having a lot to offer. Clearly, they are more likely to feel *resentment* than fear because they see themselves as able to control their own fate no matter what the organisation does. They feel insulted or offended at not being consulted, rather than fear. Such employees can be your worst enemies if you impose change on them: they either leave or lead a concerted resistance movement. Either way, you lose.

➲ **How you approach coping with change yourself or helping others to change should, therefore, take account of whether fear or resentment is most likely to underlie resistance.**

As we have seen, we need to understand the role of self-esteem. Everyone will suffer bouts of low self-esteem. It is not a permanent condition like height – except for a minority of people. Most of us will be in a state of low self-esteem from time to time.

Overcoming the resenters

The resenters are easier to deal with than those with low self-esteem. Involvement is essential for them and it should take two forms:

● participation in deciding what and how to change, and
● taking part in a pilot project.

There is nothing like first-hand experience with something new to see that it's not so bad after all. It is not often practical to involve a lot of employees in planning change, but trying it out on a pilot basis is a better selling approach anyway. The easy route of simply more and clearer communication about the reasons for the change may only increase resentment.

HOW YOUR SELF-ESTEEM AFFECTS YOUR RESISTANCE TO CHANGE

To get to grips with resistance to change, therefore, a good place to start is to check whether you have a high level of self-esteem or not.

➡ **Self-esteem is a matter of seeing yourself as having a high level of value, of being self-confident and feeling that you have some control over your own destiny.**

Like change, self-esteem is also in the eye of the beholder in the sense that we compare ourselves to others either favourably or negatively. Healthy self-esteem would involve having as high an opinion of yourself as you do of your peers. Complete the questionnaire, *Your self-esteem* (see Figure 1.5 overleaf), to determine how you feel about yourself.

If you plan to ask your subordinates to complete this questionnaire, don't presume they will answer it honestly. We are all pretty defensive about admitting to others that we have low self-esteem. The lower your self-esteem, the more you may feel a need to protect yourself by denying it. It might help to ask them to fill it out for themselves with no expectation that they will be asked to share the results with you.

If you answered 'true' to four or fewer of these statements, your self-esteem may be on the low side. You probably have a moderate level of self-esteem if you answered 'true' to somewhere between five and eight of these statements. Finally, your self-esteem is likely to be high if you answered 'true' to nine or more statements.

If your self-esteem is low, you may still resent change, but you will fear it as well – especially the deeper you get into it. On the other hand, if your self-esteem is quite high, it is unlikely you will fear change – either in advance or during it. Your predominant attitude

YOUR SELF-ESTEEM

		True	False
1.	I generally feel more competent than my peers.	☐	☐
2.	I usually feel that I can achieve whatever I want.	☐	☐
3.	Whatever happens to me is mostly in my control.	☐	☐
4.	I hardly every worry about how things will work out.	☐	☐
5.	I am confident that I can deal with most situations.	☐	☐
6.	I rarely doubt my ability to solve problems.	☐	☐
7.	I rarely feel guilty for asking others to do things.	☐	☐
8.	I am rarely upset by criticism.	☐	☐
9.	If I fail, it is due to circumstances, not my ability.	☐	☐
10.	I am very optimistic about my future.	☐	☐
11.	I feel that I have quite a lot to offer an employer.	☐	☐
12.	I rarely dwell for very long on personal setbacks.	☐	☐

Fig 1.5

to imposed change is more likely to be one of anger and resentment – indignation that anyone should dare to treat you with such little respect.

So, who do you blame?

The lower your self-esteem, the more you will tend to blame *yourself* rather than the organisation for your inability to adjust to change comfortably. If you tend to berate yourself for perceived failings then you will lash yourself even more viciously as you perceive your discomfort with a particular change initiative. A downward spiral may then set in, consisting of alternating decreases in your adaptability and your self-esteem. In the worst eventuality, you may hang on quite rigidly to familiar routines or become too depressed to function at all.

In the remainder of this chapter, we will focus on seeing what can be done to help people with lower self-esteem combat their fear and resistance to change.

Is there room in your organisation for those with low self-esteem?

You might be tempted to simply dismiss employees with low self-esteem, but most organisations today recognise the importance of diversity for innovation. Many creative employees are sensitive and introspective. As they do not get quite as much external feedback as their more extroverted colleagues, they can suffer more from lower self-esteem. Organisations with a premium on creativity cannot afford to hire only clones of their most outgoing employees. This is not to say that extroverted people do not experience low self-esteem. The sheer pace of change and the competition among employees to excel is bound to tax the self-esteem of everyone. As a result, fear of change based on lower self-esteem could cut across all levels and personality types within your organisation.

Organisations with a premium on creativity cannot afford to hire only clones of their most outgoing employees.

What are people afraid of?

Fear is likely to take different forms for different people and especially for different age groups. We will look at the fears of older employees in Chapter 4.

Fear felt by employees with low self-esteem

Younger and mid-career employees with low, or at best moderate, self-esteem strive to prove themselves and to be accepted. They might attach themselves to a certain way of doing things or a particular person who they identify with and who has been supportive up to now. The lower their self-esteem the more firmly they will attach themselves to whatever gives them the sense of security they are seeking. Their predominant fear is one of loss, of losing their source of security.

Suppose you attach yourself too closely to your boss and you hear a rumour that he is about to move on or be replaced. In this case you feel a sudden shock of fear over whether you will be able to adjust to someone new. Upon the arrival of your new boss, you may show your disappointment too visibly, thereby risking being seen as not fitting in to the new team.

Or perhaps you have managed to prove yourself and become accepted by mastering a difficult task or technology. This acceptance boosts your self-esteem a little, but you are never quite sure of your hold on things. So, in spite of being well-regarded for what you can do, you drive yourself to be even better at it. And then suddenly you learn that this way of doing things is to be replaced. Again you immediately feel fear with regard to your ability to re-establish yourself with the new technology. Your first thought may be one of dismay but you are likely to be soon scheming to avoid the changes or hoping they will not happen.

We noted earlier that fear of change is a function of the amount you have invested in the status quo. Employees with lower self-esteem are more likely to invest a lot of themselves too closely in a narrow range of things. This is because they tend to consolidate their hold on whatever provides them with this security instead of diversifying across several avenues of skill or relationship. They acquire an identity as the person who does X or as the associate of Y. The more firmly they become this person, the more fearful they will be of change because, most of all, they fear having to start over again. It was too frightening and stressful striving to attach themselves to their current identity in the first place and they do not want to have to go through it again.

WHAT TO DO ABOUT FEAR OF CHANGE

To lower your fear of change, you should proceed on two fronts:

- take steps to raise your self-esteem generally, and
- work to diversify yourself so that you do not invest too much in any one way of doing things.

1. Steps to raising self-esteem

There are at least four steps you can take to raise your self-esteem:

- ➡ do an audit of your strengths, both personal and professional
- ➡ obtain wider feedback, regularly
- ➡ change the way you talk to yourself
- ➡ cast off the tyranny of the SHOULDS (see below).

This discussion is based, in part, on the excellent book entitled *Self-Esteem*, by Matthew Mackay and Patrick Fanning (New Harbinger Publications, 1987).

Auditing your strengths, both personal and professional

One of the major reasons people have low self-esteem is that they feel they have no significant strengths. They see themselves as unable to offer much of any worth or value to anyone. We learn to feel this way about ourselves because we are so used to getting negative feedback for mistakes we make and so little praise for a job well done. We also tend to take what we can do well for granted. Developing a new product, for example, seems so easy to you that you don't see it as a particular strength. A good first step in raising your self-esteem, therefore, is to get a clearer idea of your strengths.

Everyone has more personal and professional strengths than they realise.

To obtain a better understanding of your strengths, it is essential to talk through all the sorts of things you have done over the past few years with a disinterested third party, someone who is a good listener. It is also vital to avoid discounting what the other person is labelling as a strength for you. You will be tempted to say 'That's just my job. That's not a strength.' So you need to avoid this temptation if you are to gain a realistic appreciation of what you have to offer. If you feel slightly embarrassed when someone is singing your praises, this may be because you don't feel you deserve such praise. But, again this feeling is itself a function of your low self-esteem. You are accustomed to getting mainly negative feedback from others (and from yourself) so you cannot believe anyone could genuinely think so well of you.

> ⮑ **The key is to listen to yourself and your own defences as well as the person who is trying to help you to better understand your strengths.**

This exercise should help you to see that you have much more to offer and to feel proud about than you thought. Still, however, you may have some residual doubts. You will wonder what other people think, whether they would be so nice to you as this person facing you, whether they would be more 'honest' if they gave you feedback anonymously.

Obtain wider feedback, regularly

Without feedback, it is all too easy to imagine the worst. We compare ourselves with others, but unfortunately we compare how *we feel inside* with *how they behave*. As most people can put up a good front most of the time, we are comparing our negative feelings about ourselves with their *apparent* good feelings about themselves. We cannot readily see that they may have the same lowish self-esteem we are experiencing. This apparent discrepancy drives our self-esteem even lower. In this state of mind we are naturally afraid of feedback because we think it will only confirm our worst opinions of ourselves. This is the only logical explanation of why most managers and other employees are so surprised, embarrassed and a little sceptical when they receive an anonymous feedback report from a group of colleagues. That is, the feedback is nearly always more positive than they were expecting.

> ⮑ **This shows that more people experience lowish self-esteem than they would admit, even to themselves.**

Still, objective feedback, no matter how fearful it seems, is better than remaining in a state of fear and self-doubt. At first, you may have to take it on faith that most employees do get more positive feedback than they expect. This will be especially true of employees with low or marginal self-esteem. It is only those with overly bloated self-esteem who get feedback that is less favourable than the flattering image they have of themselves.

Naturally, like everyone, you too will get some negative feedback, but if you keep the whole picture in perspective, you cannot help but feel gratified by the positive feedback you were not expecting.

> *The key is to celebrate your strengths, and to take positive steps to improve in the areas where fine tuning is recommended.*

The key is to celebrate your strengths, as acknowledged by the anonymous survey completed by your colleagues, and to take positive steps to improve in the areas where fine tuning is recommended. This process at least gives you some concrete specifics to work on which is much better than the totally nebulous feeling that you are no good for anything. That in itself can be very reassuring.

Change the way you talk to yourself

Receiving negative feedback all our lives for mistakes leads us to talk to ourselves negatively as well. How often do you say to yourself:

> *What an idiot!*
> *How can you be so stupid!*
> *Can't you get anything right!*
> *What a loser!*
> *There you go again!*
> *You're not really up to it, are you?!*

If you criticise yourself this harshly, it is probably because someone in your past has addressed you in this manner. While you cannot change your past, you can change the way you talk to yourself. The first thing to do is to catch yourself at it. Then you should exclaim to yourself: 'Stop it!' At this point, you should review the many good things you have done in your life and recite your list of recently highlighted strengths. Convince yourself that you do your best and that you are fundamentally O.K. But maybe you had such high standards drummed into your head that you feel that you can never be quite good enough. This means that you are a victim of the tyranny of the 'SHOULDS'.

Beware the tyranny of the SHOULDS!

Victims of the tyranny of the SHOULDS beat themselves continually with exhortations to be better at everything. They are never satisfied with anything they achieve. Nothing they do is ever good enough to satisfy them, probably because nothing was ever good enough to win the approval of their parents. So they constantly whip themselves with the command...

25

I SHOULD…

> *…be earning much more money*
> *…be the best provider in the world for my family*
> *…be at the very top of my profession*
> *…get all my work done on time always*
> *…never make any mistakes…ever*
> *…always make the right decisions*
> *…always know exactly what to do*
> *…always feel enthusiastic and energetic*
> *…always win all my arguments with everyone*
> *…always be on top of everything.*

Clearly, excessively high standards can never be met and are a sure recipe for low self-esteem. Casting off the SHOULDS does not mean having no standards, it is just being willing to accept less than perfection, aligning your standards with the level most other people find to be good enough. Easier said that done no doubt, but you will not raise your self-esteem by continually driving yourself harder to achieve your own standards – because they are insatiable – but by being more realistic.

2. Diversify yourself to avoid over-investment in the status quo

We said that raising your self-esteem was one way of reducing the fear of change. The other key is to avoid tying your identity too closely with any one way of doing things. You may see yourself as having had quite a varied career to date, but perhaps you have done a lot of the same things, just in different contexts. Have you tried challenging yourself to develop a list of the things you most like doing and asked yourself what would you least like to stop doing? Are the things you most enjoy running like a thread throughout your otherwise varied career?

➲ **To vary your portfolio of skills, you do not need to give up your favourite activities, but you should force yourself to take on responsibilities that have been foreign to you thus far.**

Expose yourself to roles you think you cannot handle. If the risk is too great, get some limited exposure first by being a member of a cross-functional team. The point is to develop an immunity to change by forcing yourself to adapt to quite different roles as often as it is feasible to do so. You may not want to change everything dear to your identity all at once. Changing organisations and functions at the same time is not a good idea. As with self-esteem enhancement, diversification is a long-term strategy for minimising your fear of change.

You can also broaden your identity by redefining what you do, as did the man in the well-known story about the floor sweeper at NASA who thought of himself not just as a cleaner but as a contributor to putting a man on the moon.

SO WHERE DOES ALL THIS LEAVE US?

In our efforts to cope better with change and to help others adjust more happily, it is essential to do what we can to enhance self-esteem – our own and that of others.

➲ **Self-esteem enhancement is no quick fix recipe for managing change. It is a long-term strengthening process to help all employees take more control over the faster pace of change we can expect in the new millennium.**

The higher your self-esteem, and the less you are wedded to any one way of working, the less problematic will be your fear of change. And if you do not fear change, you will find it easier to adapt when it hits you unexpectedly.

PRACTICAL STEPS

➡ Audit yourself to see whether you fear or resent change.

➡ If you fear change, take steps to raise your self-esteem.

➡ If you resent change, be sure you are not overly invested in today.

➡ If you resent change, push yourself to get more closely involved with it as you cannot learn to like it at arm's length – first-hand exposure is the best recipe for overcoming resentment.

➡ If you are indifferent to change, try to immunise yourself by changing a few things you would not want to change; ensure regular moves outside your comfort zone.

SUMMARY

This chapter has been mainly about resistance to change based on fear. Managers who fear change are concerned about losing ground in their own personal race to stay on top of their lives. Excessive fear of change is related to low self-esteem but there are a few practical steps you can take to enhance your self-esteem. We also touched on resistance to change based on resentment. Managers who resent change have higher self-esteem and imposed change makes them angry rather than afraid. It is important to distinguish between resistance to imposed change and the willing, but often futile, effort to break bad habits. Imposed change and the resentment it causes is the subject of Chapter 2.

'Nothing is ever done in this world until men are prepared to kill one another if it is not done.'

George Bernard Shaw, *Major Barbara*

CHAPTER

THE INDIGNITY OF IMPOSED CHANGE

OBJECTIVE
- To shed some light on why managers resent change, how it relates to their identity, how their defensiveness can undermine their ability to adapt and how to see change as an opportunity instead of a disaster.

INTRODUCTION

We all know a few change-related war stories, accompanied by casualties. They all revolve around the suddenness of managers being blown out of their jobs. Like the senior executive who arrived back from holiday to find his office occupied by someone else. 'Why didn't anybody tell me?' he asked, in vain. The most common complaint is precisely that: 'If only I had been given some warning, I could have prepared for this.'

But the organisation needs key people to keep performing up to the day they are asked to leave or are offered a demotion, so how can they say, three months in advance, 'Oh, by the way, we are planning to move you out of your job in awhile, but we will give you the details later.'

You may be thinking that most organisational changes are not this dramatic. When managers are asked to leave, there is no problem of resistance to change – they simply have no choice in the matter. The drama may not be so visible for most organisational changes, but those on the receiving end can feel just as shocked and disorientated.

In this chapter, we will discuss the varying severity of different types of imposed change in terms of how great the impact is likely to be on you or your employees. We will then use this discussion, along with the ideas we looked at in the last chapter on resistance to change, to suggest some ways of increasing our adaptability.

SHAKING UP YOUR IDENTITY

Even restricting ourselves to *imposed* change in this chapter, rather than discussing initiated changes as well, we are still left with two main topics:

- preparing ourselves so that we can adjust more comfortably when faced with unwelcome changes in the future, and
- coping with imposed change after the fact.

For the moment, we will focus on the former issue: preparing to adapt more readily.

Imposed versus self-initiated change

It is important to distinguish between imposed and self-initiated change. It is easy to see why imposed change can be difficult to accept, but you may think that you would have no problem adjusting to changes you initiate yourself. We will focus here on imposed change and consider self-initiated change in Chapter 5, but a word or two on the latter may be useful here if only to convince you that it is not always very easy.

There are two ways in which self-initiated changes can be hard. One is when you cannot make up your mind to initiate a change. For example, you may be offered a promotion, but to a different country that you are not too keen to live in. So, you let yourself get stuck in an agonising state of indecision for months. The decision to retire is often a self-initiated change and one of the most difficult. These are examples of self-initiated changes where the difficulty occurs *before* the change is made and which prevents or delays your decision to make the change.

The second form of self-initiated change that can cause resistance and can be an agonising struggle is where you readily take the plunge, only to realise *after* you have made the change how difficult it is to adjust. Let's say you jumped at the chance to take a promotion to a different country, but then could not settle into the new location. Another good example of this is any promotion – especially one that takes you to a new employer. A classic struggle to adapt is surely the battle to fit into a new role in a different organisation with a different culture where you have to build a new support group from scratch. Yet what could be more self-initiated?

Self-initiated changes are, however, in principle, easier to cope with than imposed changes so long as you have 'immunised' yourself by making frequent changes throughout your career. We will discuss self-initiated change later. For now we need to try to get a better handle on imposed change and how to cope with it.

How to cope with imposed change

There is little doubt that the hardest imposed changes to deal with for most managers are those that require them to give up something that is central to their identities. For many it will be their role, status or some other aspect of their role that is critical to how they see themselves. Less central will be organisational procedures or processes that they have no personal stake in maintaining.

In the last chapter, we concluded that the more your identity is bound up with the way things are, the more threatened you will feel about any change that undermines your familiar patterns. The concentric circles in Figure 2.1 depict the varying degrees of centrality to our identity of various organisational arrangements. What you put in each concentric circle will be unique to you.

➲ **The key point is for you to take stock for yourself of what is most central and most peripheral for you.**

Whatever is most central for you will be the hardest for you to give up. You will be less bothered about losing what is of more peripheral importance to you.

Suppose you identify most closely with your current role and this happens to be the role of a change agent. So, you ask, how could I have trouble with change? If you identify with being a change agent then being asked to assume a maintenance or caretaker role would be just the type of change you might have most difficulty accepting. In such a role you would have to pay close attention to detail and efficiency – not usually the favourite activity of change agents. This change would, in other words, undermine your identity and self-esteem.

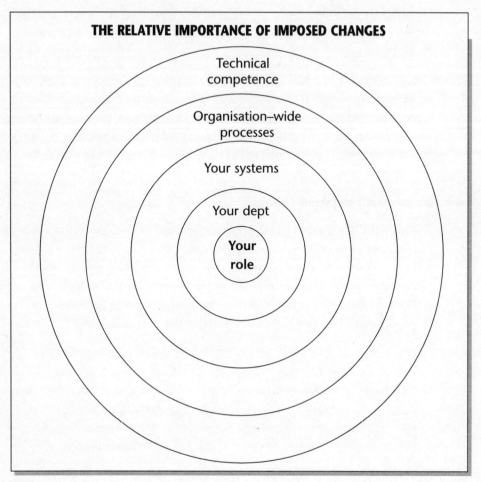

Fig 2.1

What does your identity revolve around?

What aspect of your work or personal life would it most disturb you to give up? What would you least like to change about your current work/life patterns? Rank in order the items listed in the questionnaire, *What is central to your identity?* (see Figure 2.2), putting 1 for what is high or most important to you and 18 for what is low or least important for you. The difficulty with ranking these priorities for yourself is that you may not realise how central they are unless they were taken away from you. So you will have to try to imagine yourself living without what is currently important to you.

WHAT IS CENTRAL TO YOUR IDENTITY?

Rank order

1. My status in the organisational hierarchy. ☐
2. The particular initiatives I have implemented. ☐
3. My technical/functional competence. ☐
4. My reputation and skill as a manager. ☐
5. The present organisation of my department. ☐
6. Reporting to my current boss. ☐
7. The specific role I currently occupy. ☐
8. The particular products/services we now offer. ☐
9. My daily/monthly routines. ☐
10. The people/team I now work with. ☐
11. Contact with outsiders – customers/suppliers. ☐
12. My life outside the organisation. ☐
13. My reputation as a major force for change. ☐
14. The strategic direction we are now pursuing. ☐
15. The specific processes that seem to work well. ☐
16. My unique knowledge of our business/markets. ☐
17. Being recognised as competent relative to others. ☐
18. Being a member of my profession. ☐
19. Other? ☐

Note: If you decide to complete the 'Other?' item then rank all items 1 to 19 and not 1 to 18.

Fig 2.2

If you decide that it is your role that you identify most closely with, it may not be clear, even after doing the above questionnaire, whether it is the role itself in some all-encompassing sense or some aspect of your role – like the influence you have, your status in the organisation, your role's importance for key strategic results, the remuneration associated with the position or some other feature – that is important.

➲ **It is because our role is so important to us that some organisations 'kick people upstairs' as a way of removing them from their current jobs if they are not performing as desired. In fact, they are 'promoted' to a position in which they are effectively sidelined, but being a 'promotion', it has a certain face-saving value. And that is the key point.**

ROLES AT RISK

Clearly, particular roles are most at risk of becoming obsolete in the future. Any number of changes yet unknown are sure to require organisations to continually restructure themselves, forcing all managers to adopt new roles. The closer you identify with a particular role, therefore, the more at risk you are of having to adapt to unexpected and imposed change.

This problem should be gradually declining as many organisations move away from roles conceived as narrow boxes. Not only is it dangerous to identify too closely with a *particular* role, the whole idea of occupying any role at all may soon be obsolete for many of us. Managers are already increasingly required to 'float' between various functions with less well-defined boundaries. Many are uncomfortable with this ambiguity and complain of a loss of efficiency, although such complaining is partly defensive as well as partly rational.

Managers, as yet, seem to find it hard to see this evolving state of affairs in a positive light. The advantage of such role ambiguity is that you should be better prepared to change roles when required. The positive attitude to role ambiguity is to see it as an opportunity (rather than as a threat) to expand and diversify yourself even further. You should now see yourself as free to create your own 'services' to offer your employer, just as you would if you were a self-employed contractor to your organisation.

➲ **The main point here is to shift your identity away from anything that has a high obsolescence risk associated with it – and roles are about as high risk as you can get.**

Even if you are presently in quite a tightly-defined role, where there is little ambiguity, you can still redefine how you think of your role. Instead of thinking of yourself as a Marketing Director or Operations Director, redefine your role so that you stop thinking of yourself as an X and begin to think of yourself as a professional who adds value in certain ways. For example, instead of saying, 'I am a Systems Engineer', you might say, 'I am a professional who adds value by devising and/or maintaining various production or information management processes.' This is a bit of a mouthful but it is also broader, allowing you to encompass a wider range of activities, so as these change, your role, as you now conceive it, stays the same.

You might object that the danger of this way of coping with change is that employees are encouraged to think of their roles so broadly that we will reach a point where nobody feels they have any specific accountabilities or sense of commitment and, as a consequence, performance will slide. What then of the benefit of cultivating broader occupational identities? The idea behind this move is that one way of coping with rapid change is to find something that remains the same through change, an anchor that can provide us with an ongoing sense of who we are across major changes. This issue is similar to the dilemma of whether to be a generalist versus a technical specialist. The danger of over-specialisation is, of course, the risk of obsolescence again. The same issue crops up at the organisational level in terms of whether to major on a narrow range of products or to diversify. Diversification is an insurance policy that applies equally at the individual and organisational levels.

Diversification is an insurance policy that applies equally at the individual and organisational levels.

With all of these issues the key is to get the balance right for yourself. To best prepare yourself for change, you need to broaden your identity while at the same time adding quite specific value at any given time. The trick for the individual manager is to constantly strive to get the balance right between specialisation and diversification.

➲ Having options will give you a greater chance of avoiding a sense of devastation if one option becomes a dead end.

Seeing yourself as a technical specialist

Increasingly, employees are less enthusiastic about managerial roles anyway. Many are reluctant to abandon their technical specialty. They are learning that the status of the knowledge worker is rising and managerial functions are being built into their jobs. But technical specialists are at great risk in the face of rapid change. As knowledge in any given area becomes even more complex, every specialty that exists today will sub-divide again and again, creating specialisations within specialisations. Just as employees need to diversify and broaden their identities in order to be more adaptable in the face of change, at the same time the pressure to specialise to an even greater extent is also increasing. The only way to keep up with an ever-expanding technical field is to pursue its developments into ever-greater detail as it emerges.

The only escape from this downward spiral into ever-increasing, and potentially dead end, specialisation is for each employee to become more entrepreneurial. This means keeping an eye on where their own broader market is moving. You then need to adapt just ahead of any crisis in your field. For example, if you specialised in refining the electric typewriter in the 1970s, you should have started developing skills in the personal computer field by the mid-1980s at the latest. Otherwise, you are probably out of work by now. This means cultivating some skills in broader market analysis and in how to run your own entrepreneurial business – all this on top of your technical specialisation. The challenge for the human resource specialist here is to teach employees these skills and to ensure that they are fully able to manage their own careers in this entrepreneurial way.

SHADES OF IMPOSITION

Most of the changes we will have to face in our lifetimes will not be of our own choosing. To manage these changes as best we can we have to improve our adaptability in two ways:

- prepare ourselves, in advance, to be more receptive to change, and
- adjust to change after the fact.

Preparing to be more receptive to change

The issue to discuss at this point is how to prepare ourselves for imposed change. We will look at the difficulty of responding after the fact to imposed change and the problem of self-initiated change later, in Chapter 5.

Types of imposed change

There are two ways in which change can be imposed on us. One is when our organisational superiors directly decide to change some aspect of our role – like splitting it in two, for instance. The second source of change occurs in the business environment, beyond anyone's direct control, but it forces us to make unwelcome changes in any case. An example of environmental change would be the development of new technology or services by our competitors that forces us to follow suit, thereby making our role superfluous – at least as we are currently performing it.

Even some of the changes imposed directly on us by our superiors will really be caused by changes in the environment. If we are managing a particular service that the organisation must abandon because of competitive pressure it is not simply a whim on our boss's part.

Delegation and change

Some imposed changes are very subtle, like staying in your current role but gaining some broader responsibilities. A broader focus may force you to delegate more of your favoured day-to-day activities. Despite the apparent subtlety of such a change, it can still cause significant identity upsets if you feel too much personal ownership over these activities. The line between imposed and self-initiated change becomes a fine one in such an example. Despite the pressure to delegate more, it is really up to us whether we let go of some of our favourite activities or hold onto them. What has delegation got to do with change, you ask? But getting

41

promoted is in fact a major change for most of us. And too many managers are not all that happy about delegating. Their reluctance is not often seen as a type of resistance to change, but that is surely what it is.

Why is it that so many managers simply cannot let go of cherished aspects of their role even when they should be focusing on higher-value-added activities? The usual rationalisations for not adjusting to the need to delegate revolve around the following alleged problems:

- not having anyone competent enough to delegate to
- having subordinates that are already overburdened, and
- a felt need to make sure that things are done properly.

Resistance to delegation can be justified by a line of reasoning that in fact turns out to be a self-fulfilling prophecy. You tell yourself that none of your subordinates can handle your responsibilities and you show such a lack of faith in their abilities that you actually undermine their confidence to do the job. So they either check with you obsessively before making the slightest move or they fail through lack of confidence, thereby confirming your initial judgement.

Or you argue that they are already too overloaded and so you cannot impose on them any more work. But if you do not delegate fully, this means that you are expecting your subordinates to stay abreast of the detail you are keeping your nose in. Otherwise, how will they be able to answer your detailed questions at the drop of a hat? This means that they cannot delegate very much either, so again justifying your defensive arguments.

➲ **The first step in adapting to delegating more effectively is to set aside your rationalisations and admit that delegation is something of a challenge for you.**

> **Without doubt it is some type of fear that is preventing you from delegating more fully.**

If you are having trouble delegating, you might like to use this difficulty as an opportunity to improve your ability to adapt to change more generally. Think of your issue with delegation as a microcosm of broader organisational changes. Because you can control what happens in this microcosm, you can use it to experiment on yourself, to stretch yourself in terms of adaptability. Without doubt it is some type of fear that is preventing you from delegating more fully.

Think about the following questions.

What are you afraid of?

1. That you are not really competent in your new responsibilities, so hanging onto your old duties gives you a sense of accomplishment?

2. That your boss will ask you questions that you cannot answer unless you are personally on top of everything?

3. That you will be dispensable if you are not doing more than your share?

I suspect that number 1 underlies the other reasons, and any other you can think of, for not delegating. Other reasons are therefore just defensive rationalisations. Suppose you have just been promoted. Naturally, whether you can admit it to yourself or not, you are probably somewhat worried that you will not be able to live up to your boss's expectations in your new role. Hanging on to your old duties is a way of reassuring yourself that you can do something well. Your new job contains a lot more ambiguity, simply because it is unfamiliar to you. Ambiguity is scary to most people because it means being out of control. So you spend too much time doing your old job instead of delegating to your successor to ensure that you feel in control of something.

A form of regression is involved in this process. When we get angry and start yelling and screaming, we are regressing under pressure to a more childish way of behaving. Regression in this context means abandoning the cultural control of emotion that we are supposed to have learned as we grew up. The pressure and anxiety of the moment cause us to regress in this manner. Similarly, due to the anxiety of change when we are promoted, we regress to what is more familiar to us. So instead of facing our ambiguous higher level duties, we find excuses to keep doing our old job. Whether you have just been promoted or not, if you are like most people, you will revert to doing what you do best under pressure simply because that is your comfort zone. Usually this is some lower-level task that calls upon your functional skills rather than your managerial competence: hence *poor delegation*.

If you can face this fear in yourself, let go of your old job, and tackle the scary ambiguity of your new job head on, your change experiment will have succeeded.

➲ **It may help to write down all the reasons you would offer for not delegating and to ask yourself how they might be rationalisations.**

If you have no one to delegate to, how easy would you find it if you did have someone?

If you can make this change yourself, it would also be useful to document how you felt in focusing more fully on your new job and how you managed to cope with that ambiguity and the loss of your familiar sources of accomplishment and reassurance. This self-analysis should then help you to consolidate your new-found adaptability and make you better able to adapt to imposed changes in the future.

DEFENSIVENESS AND FACE-SAVING IN ADJUSTING TO CHANGE

To clarify how imposed change affects us, it may be helpful to look at what is the most difficult change to accept. Surely, the hardest change to accept is a change to your role based on unsatisfactory performance. If your performance is totally unacceptable you will probably be asked to leave the organisation altogether, or you will be kicked upstairs. On the other hand, if some aspects of your contribution are still highly valued, then your imposed role change will be sold to you as an 'opportunity' of some sort. While this 'packaging' is an attempt to help you save face, your ability to cope with change is partly a function of how able you are to see such changes as opportunities.

Nevertheless, you are likely to feel varying degrees of hurt and anger. Regardless of how well the organisation has positioned the change in a face-saving manner, you will contribute some face-saving moves of your own. In part, this is a healthy form of defensiveness that we must use in order to cope with the harshest of life's realities. It is the psychological complement to your immune system for warding off physical disease. Defensiveness is only a problem when it leads us to live in an imaginary world, failing to face reality at all.

➲ **This abuse of normal defensiveness is a common way of resisting change.**

The importance of saving face

We talked about rationalisation as a way of avoiding the real reasons why we don't delegate. This is a form of counter-productive defensiveness. While it is necessary to protect ourselves against severe hurt, some defensiveness is simply self-defeating. Like taking a pill that does no more for us than mask our symptoms, a lot of defensive behaviour is just a quick fix that allows us to avoid facing reality and put off having to resolve our problems on a longer-term basis.

Defensiveness in its milder forms – what we call *saving face* – is not always counter-productive. It is actually a very important and essential change management skill. We all need it to protect ourselves against severe blows to our self-esteem and change agents should cultivate the skill of helping others save face if they expect to excel at managing change. By saving face, whether your own or someone else's, the exposure to an otherwise humiliating reality is made softer and less public. Face-saving enables you, or the other person, to move on more gracefully without having so openly to admit some form of failure or defeat. Change agents often fail because they do not take account of how wedded emotionally people are to existing arrangements and no attempt is therefore made to help them save face.

> *By saving face, whether your own or someone else's, the exposure to an otherwise humiliating reality is made softer and less public.*

We may wonder what saving face amounts to because we all do it so automatically that we may have difficulty thinking of examples. But you are saving your face whenever you present an unpalatable imposed change in a more positive light. When you say that you wanted to make this change yourself but just hadn't got around to it yet, you are saving face. Tactless colleagues are good at laughing at you by exposing your feeble efforts to cover up your anger and humiliation at being forced to give up a favoured status.

➲ **Good change agents should be skilled in helping you save face rather than leaving you to improvise for yourself or, worse, making it difficult for you to save face.**

If you are unable to save face because the imposed change is too major or too public, your anger and resentment are likely to lead to a stronger and less productive form of defensiveness. Defending yourself against a painful setback may then take the form of a counter-attack, even if it only occurs within your own head. A purely subjective counter-attack could take the form of questioning (to yourself) the sanity of someone who could make such a stupid decision as to change your role in this way.

More overt defensiveness may take the form of simply denying the change and you may then carry on as if nothing has happened. Or you may resolve to sabotage the change in some way, by spreading unrest or more subtly undermining the change.

EXAMPLE

You might find all sorts of reasons why a proposed organisation-wide change should not apply to your department. What you may not realise is that you are being very creative in thinking up these reasons and in downplaying the good reasons in favour of the change. It is hard to admit that this is defensiveness due to hurt pride rather than, as you see it, simply a rational rejection of an inappropriate initiative.

Failure to help employees save face is often the reason why change agents create more resistance than they had to relieve in the first place. Of course, the change agent's face-saving move for failing to implement a change successfully is to blame the stubborn employees.

Getting the boot

Saving face is hardest for managers who get fired. Being asked to leave your organisation altogether is clearly the hardest and most traumatic of changes to be asked to accept. Understanding how managers react to this imposed change may shed some light on how they react to less dramatic changes. If you find yourself in this situation, you may be provided with job search counselling. Your counsellor will help you develop, what they call in this profession, the 'leaving story'. Your leaving story must be as honest as possible, one that your ex-boss will corroborate, but one that does not put you in a very damaging light. An explanation along the lines of the organisation changing direction and not being able to put your talents to best use any longer is the usual thrust of the leaving story.

How to explain their departure in a face saving manner is one of the main worries of managers following a forced exit: what are they going to tell prospective future employers? The leaving story is equally important – if not more important – to help the manager come to terms with the blow him or herself. Clearly, therefore, imposed departures go beyond other role changes in terms of how damaging they are to the manager's self-esteem and identity.

EXAMPLE

A forced exit is, in a sense, an example of resistance to change because you resist it in your mind. You may even succeed in convincing yourself that you were planning to leave anyway and that this may be the best opportunity to have come your way in a long time. There is clearly a fine line between this way of reasoning being a healthy way to face the future, on the one hand, and an otherwise unproductive denial of reality.

The point of this discussion is to highlight how important the leaving story is to managers who are asked to leave the organisation. The leaving story is a face-saving exercise. In the context of being fired, such face-saving is not a matter of counterproductive defensiveness, it is rather an essential step to recovering sufficient self-esteem to carry on and to be able to present yourself to prospective new employers with any degree of confidence. The critical point here is that this need for face-saving is completely transparent to outplacement counsellors in this situation. The high visibility of this strong human need only reinforces how important, if less visible, it is in coping with less traumatic changes within the organisation as well.

Less drastic role changes can produce just as much resistance to change, both mentally and in the way you behave on the job.

EXAMPLE

You may take covert action to undermine your successor if you are moved aside or asked to split your duties with someone else. Chaos can result if a manager simply goes on as before, totally ignoring the reshuffled duties. Having two managers claiming the same territory is undoubtedly very confusing to the rest of the organisation, not to mention very costly.

Resisting broader organisational changes

It is clearly easier to resist or avoid changes in organisational processes that do not bear so directly on your role. The key problem organisations have with change is the tendency for people to resist large-scale changes of direction. A good deal of this resistance is not even based on hostile intentions. It is often simply the difficulty of breaking bad habits – such as smoking, for instance. Many employees are genuinely excited about a new direction, but honestly cannot avoid slipping back into old habits after a period of trying to adapt to the change. Although such change may be imposed by competitive conditions, many willing employees will see such change as at least partly self-initiated. Similarly, trying to quit smoking may be forced by health considerations but it is also largely self-initiated. Unfortunately that doesn't make it any easier.

Managers intent on resisting change are well aware of the fact that old habits die hard.

Managers intent on resisting change are well aware of the fact that old habits die hard. They know that if they just stick to their favoured ways of doing things long enough the pendulum has a very strong chance of swinging back to their side. Inertia will set in and the enthusiasm for the new processes will wane. You can even take a more active part in undermining change by quietly sewing seeds of doubt in the minds of your colleagues and subtly undermining the credibility of the current change champions.

EXAMPLE

A favourite strategy for resisting organisation-wide changes is to argue that your department or division is different. And of course we all like to feel unique and special. So, if you are feeling particularly resentful, a little creativity should allow you to think of dozens of reasons why the changes should not apply to your department. If your department is quite central, your seemingly rational arguments are bound to dampen enthusiasm for the change in other departments. With any luck, your actions may cause the whole change initiative to die a quiet death in a relatively short time.

Too many change agents seem to assume that people are all basically rational and if you only explain fully and clearly the reasons for a change, everyone will see the merits of the decision and jump on the bandwagon. This is clearly naive as it neglects the psychology of self-esteem and identity. But even if you go one step further and involve people in planning the change, that doesn't mean that the change will be any easier to carry off than other major changes in personal lifestyle – like quitting smoking.

Being less counter-productively defensive

If you are to be successful in preparing yourself for imposed and inevitable change, then it is essential to learn to react to change less defensively.

EXAMPLE

Suppose that you work for a large software company with an international reputation. Suppose also that some of your competitors are single-person entrepreneurial firms. Imagine, finally, that changes in your common market are forcing your organisation to make similar changes in its product portfolio.

Now compare yourself, as a manager in the large organisation, with a sole proprietor, an entrepreneurial business person, one who is a direct competitor of your organisation. When the market changes for the entrepreneur, he can feel defeated. But the more successful entrepreneur will be quick to see such change as an opportunity to develop and sell some new services. The effective entrepreneur is excited by such opportunities, not angry and resentful like managers in large organisations often are when faced by similar market changes. Why the radically different attitude? Why should you feel shocked, dismayed and betrayed while the entrepreneur does not experience these feelings?

The problem is that you, the manager, see imposed change as somehow a *personal* attack whereas the entrepreneur sees it as nothing to do with him personally. Part of your sense of identity and self-esteem hinges on feeling a part of the overall management team. To be told to change is, in effect, to be told that your say in the matter is incorrect or at least over-ruled. Not only are you being told to change your role, you are also being told, if more indirectly, that your weight in critical strategic decisions is not quite what you thought it was. Hence you are asked to absorb a double blow. The result, in any case, is that you take such changes personally, whereas the entrepreneur does not. Why is this?

Part of your identity as a manager in a large organisation is determined by your particular role, but you also identify with the organisation as a whole as well. When you speak to outsiders such as customers, suppliers, family members or acquaintances you are your organisation. This is why imposed change feels like betrayal. For you to feel this way as an entrepreneur, you would have to be a minority partner in a firm where the majority partner encouraged you to think like a full partner then turned around and made major changes without consulting you. Naturally you would feel betrayed.

The need for a scapegoat

When bad things happen to us we naturally look around to see who we can blame. Psychologists have long known that we all tend to pat ourselves on the back when something good happens to us and to blame circumstances, bad luck, the government, the weather, or some other person – anything but ourselves – when something bad happens. If you have low self-esteem, on the other hand, you may indeed blame yourself, but those of you with high self-esteem tend to look elsewhere for a culprit. We do this precisely to avoid having to lower our self-esteem. This makes blaming others a defensive move. While a degree of self-protection is a healthy way to cope, as we have seen, most defensiveness is counter-productive and self-defeating. This is so because it prevents us from really learning how to behave differently in difficult situations. Why, after all, should you do anything different if you did nothing wrong in the first place, that is, if it was someone else's fault?

What has this got to do with coping with change, you ask?

Well, if you are an entrepreneur and your market changes, you are right to look to the environment to see what happened and where the market is going. But if you are a manager in an organisation, as we have noted, your first reaction to an unwelcome change in direction is to feel anger and resentment towards those who made the decision. So you look for a scapegoat to avoid having to think that maybe your view of where the business should be going could be wrong, hence having to lower your self-esteem.

Why do we react this way?

Generally, when a disaster befalls us we wonder why it had to happen.

51

Suppose you are camping and a flash flood suddenly sweeps through your camp site. You survive but lose a loved one in the flood. In groping to alleviate your pain you tell yourself that this should not have happened. You begin to think how it could have been avoided. If only you had gone somewhere else to camp. Or if only you had listened more carefully to the weather reports. Or if only the camp site managers had warned you.

This is the same reaction as that of any person who is suddenly fired: 'Why wasn't I given any warning?' Naturally, we all want to avoid disaster, so where possible we want some warning. When disaster does strike, one of our first thoughts is often why did I not get any warning.

Now when the powers that be in your organisation announce a sudden change in direction, one that is not especially pleasant in your view, you have someone to blame, unlike the entrepreneur. You can always argue that *they* should have warned us or *they* could have delayed this decision, phased it in or, preferably, taken another, more sensible course of action altogether.

Because you have someone to blame, you take advantage of it for the simple reason that it helps you to unload some of your anger, pain and resentment. In short, it makes you feel better to have someone to blame rather than have to swallow the pain and live with it totally alone.

Learning to live with no warnings

Like all situations that annoy us, we can choose to react differently, It may not be easy, but it is possible. If you can convince yourself that such defensiveness really does undermine your ability to learn from situations, then maybe you can begin to react differently in future. If you accept that your need to unload your bad feelings is a natural human reaction, along with the desire to preserve your self-esteem, perhaps you can decide that you don't need this vent any more, that you can manage to feel good generally, and good about yourself, without needing someone else to unload upon.

➡ In practical terms, this means that the next time your superiors decide to change direction suddenly, catch yourself before you blow up and ask yourself what you would have done in their shoes. This does not mean arguing what you would have done in your shoes, but genuinely trying to see it from their point of view.

➡ It may help to suspend judgement until you have dug really deeply into the issue to unearth all the possible benefits of their chosen course of action.

➡ Psychologists have also discovered that the best way to develop a positive attitude to an unpleasant situation is to write an essay and make a presentation on all the benefits of the new way of looking at something.

Living with not always being right

Large organisations are more like national states than they are like one-person entrepreneurial businesses. Because of their size, large organisations, like states, have irreconcilably different political parties vying for power. This is inevitably a win–lose game, on many occasions, and every player, however much a partner they may feel, needs to get used to losing some of the time to competing ideas. This can make it harder to accept changes initiated by those in power if you are not among the in-group. It then becomes harder to put yourself in the position of those in power, in order to see what might be rational about their decision. Wherever there are competing political forces at work, each side naturally sees the other as the enemy. And the enemy can never be right. If the enemy is never right, how can you ever accept changes initiated by them? A tall order no doubt.

Wherever there are competing political forces at work, each side naturally sees the other as the enemy.

The only way you can rise above this situation is to tell yourself that you refuse to play this game. This is not to say that you have to stop manoeuvring to obtain greater influence, but you can perhaps, by being more aware of how your reactions are triggered, simply decide to put the interests of the organisation ahead of your own emotional reactions. If you can achieve this step, then maybe you can more readily set your initial reactions aside and see some good in the other side's decisions.

The organisational politician sees himself as competing with colleagues for degrees of influence over the organisation's strategic direction. Different metaphors will inevitably lie behind how you think of this competition for control. If you imagine yourself fighting on a battlefield, you may be inclined to think of regaining lost territory when a colleague gains some influence that you previously held. However, if you visualise yourself as climbing a ladder, instead of trying to hold a position on a battlefield, you could react quite differently. You could convince yourself that you had better jump onto the same rung of the ladder that your colleague has just jumped onto if you are to have any hope of beating him to the next rung. This attitude would then lead you to be one of the first to endorse the change. This advice seems to support a viciously competitive way of life in organisations. But it is *not* an endorsement, only an attempt to describe what is surely the reality in most organisations.

➲ **Getting closely involved with the core direction the organisation is now moving in will put you in a better position to see where to go next than you would be if you decided to fight the change from a relatively outside position.**

This is behaving just like the self-employed entrepreneur and you should thereby enhance your own creativity and that of the organisation's by your example. The problem is that too many managers tend to sulk and withdraw from the fray at this point and this makes it doubly hard to then turn around and take the 'if-you-can't-beat-them-join-them-approach'. Once such managers have publicly committed themselves to resistance, an even greater loss of face is required to then drop this, apparently, moral high ground.

In this chapter we have been discussing how to prepare yourself to deal with unexpected changes. Inevitably, some of this bears on how to react to change after the fact and we will say more about this later but, for now, here is a short list of things to do to be more adaptable.

PRACTICAL STEPS

→ Be aware of how you react to unpleasant surprises.

→ You can enhance your self-esteem even more if you can control your immediate emotional reactions.

→ Analyse your emotional reactions and reasons for resisting change to see if you can honestly chalk some of them up to counter-productive defensiveness.

→ Seek less immediately to blame others for unpleasant happenings.

→ Try, as a first reaction, to see what you can learn from setbacks.

→ When you feel annoyance, ask yourself 'In what way am I hurting myself by reacting this way and how could I look at it differently?'

→ Strike a balance between specialisation and diversification.

→ Think about what your contribution is to the organisation and redefine it so as not to tie your identity to closely to a fixed role.

→ Analyse your reasons for not delegating more fully to understand better why you are not letting go as much as perhaps you could.

→ Without giving up your attempts to win and have influence, be sure that you give opponents the occasional benefit of the doubt in the context of trying to be clear about what is best for the organisation.

SUMMARY

Managers resist change in large organisations because they see it as imposed on them. Unlike the entrepreneur, they take imposed change as a personal insult. Coping better with such change requires managers to gain a better understanding of how their emotional reactions and defensiveness get in the way of their own success and how they can instead see themselves in more entrepreneurial terms, begining to see change as an opportunity.

Chapter 3 explores the entrepreneurial approach to imposed change in more detail.

'The man who listens to Reason is lost:
Reason enslaves all those whose minds are
not strong enough to master her.'

George Bernard Shaw, *Man and Superman*

CHAPTER

3

YOUR OWN CHANGE MANAGEMENT STRATEGY

OBJECTIVES

- To encourage managers to view change as an entrepreneur would do, as a stimulating opportunity to learn and grow.

- To replace our defensive, 'rational' approach to decision making with a more open, experimental one.

INTRODUCTION

Suppose your organisation has just re-organised and your role has been split in two, with you being asked to accept the less influential half. How do you react to this personal blow? Your new role is presented to you in a face-saving manner but the loss of status and power are too obvious to hide. Not only did you lose the combined role, you also lost the best bit.

Let's say that you were Marketing and Sales Director. Your background has been in sales but you have enjoyed the more strategic aspects of the marketing function. Now, you have been asked to be just Director of Sales because a career professional marketing person is being brought in to take over this role. You naturally see this as the organisation giving you the message that you were not quite up to the marketing side of the role. The humiliating aspect of this change is knowing that most of your colleagues and subordinates see it this way as well. So how do you recover from this blow?

EASING THE TRAUMA

One popular, or at least well-known, strategy for coping with a trauma like the one above is modelled on strategies for coping with major personal tragedies, such as the death of a loved one.

Building bridges to the future

William Bridges has written two books on the subject of transition (*Transitions*, 1980, and *Managing Transitions*, 1991, both published by Addison-Wesley Publishing Company, Inc.) and has contributed a great deal to our understanding of certain kinds of transition. Bridges based his approach to transitions on theories developed in the early 1970s to help people cope with the death of a loved one. The distinguishing features of death as a transition are that it is:

● unavoidable
● generally involuntary

- often sudden, and
- well defined – there is a clear boundary between life and death.

(Bridges talks about transitions rather than change, but we needn't distinguish between the two for our purposes.)

Coping with any transition as sudden as the death of a loved one naturally falls into three stages:

- coming to terms with the loss
- a middle confusing period
- followed by acceptance and reorientation.

➲ **So, the advice to you, based on this way of looking at transitions, is first to come to terms with the loss of your position.**

Bridges sees this phase as mourning your loss. He advocates employing quite explicit rituals as part of the mourning process. For example, you could contrive a ritual burial or funeral. I'm not sure what you would bury but something symbolic of your old role should do. Because this change is personal rather than organisation-wide, you might prefer to hold your wake in the privacy of your own home. If you were involved in closing down an entire site and moving your whole office to a new location, a more public funeral might be appropriate. As it is, any public display of your personal grief would surely just add to your embarrassment.

After you have successfully buried your past, you are then in what Bridges calls 'the neutral zone'. For a while, you will be a sort of walking wounded person. No wound can be wished away. You just have to wait for it to heal. During this period, you will be confused, bewildered and uncertain as to how to even begin to move forward again.

You cannot force yourself through any of these stages, but in time, you will begin to feel an acceptance of your situation and start to reorientate yourself to it.

➲ **The main point that Bridges seems to be making is that it can help to be aware that these are normal psychological reactions to traumatic changes and that you should let yourself ride them out rather than suppress your feelings or allow yourself to do anything drastic.**

This is surely good advice for coping with any major organisational changes that approach the severity of the trauma of losing a loved one. The question is, however, are all organisational changes this traumatic?

There is no doubt that managers who are totally unprepared for a major personal blow like demotion or getting fired, will experience the sort of emotional roller-coaster ride that Bridges describes. But these are managers who should soon be a thing of the past. Managers who are this traumatised by change are usually those who have experienced little or no major change in their careers to date. Such managers are surely a nearly extinct species. Back in the 1970s when Bridges was developing his transition theory, everyone in the corporate world was reacting to rampant job loss with terrific shock and horror. Change is now a way of life, albeit still an unsettling one.

The fact of the matter is that, unlike the death of a loved one, almost any organisational change can be looked at as an *opportunity* rather than as a tragedy. This is not to make light of the very deep hurt and bewilderment that many managers continue to feel in the face of major personal change.

THE ENTREPRENEURIAL APPROACH TO CHANGE

Let's explore now how you could react differently to the demotion that we started this chapter by discussing.

There are two things you can do:

● think through how you can react differently *after the fact*, and
● make more effort to *plan* how you will accept change when it does hit you so hard in the future.

Reacting differently to the shock of personal change

In the last chapter, we briefly compared the way entrepreneurs react to change with the way managers in large organisations react. Here, we need to expand on that comparison a bit. First of all, it is necessary to acknowledge that entrepreneurs are human too. The more they expect to be able to milk a particular product line for a good while yet, the more they are likely to be shocked and disorientated by a sudden and dramatic loss of market share. In this situation, they will, no doubt, take a while to regroup. As we saw in the last chapter, however, the entrepreneur has the psychological advantage of not having anyone to blame for his plight.

The self-sufficiency of the *successful* entrepreneur should therefore make for a quick turnaround. New opportunities will be sought quickly and capitalised upon. The entrepreneur can choose to see this market change as good customer feedback. He can say 'My competitors have now committed themselves. I can take advantage of their moves to leapfrog them to the next stage of product evolution.' The entrepreneur may permit himself the luxury of a brief state of shock, but, if he really is a successful entrepreneur, he will quickly begin to think how he can take advantage of the changed market. So, there is a quick short-term reaction, followed by a longer-term pledge to further innovation, in order to regain the lead.

➡ **In short, the entrepreneur continues to behave consistently like an entrepreneur.**

In fact, the entrepreneur may not feel upset at all by such momentary setbacks. Part of the enjoyment of being an entrepreneur is to feel exhilarated by the heat of competitive battle. Otherwise it is like playing a card game with someone you can always and easily beat. What could be more boring? In business, human laziness compels us to prefer to win all the time, but always winning is the surest recipe for complacency and eventual collapse. Being on the spot in a competitive battle is just what is most attractive to entrepreneurs. Winning is really only exhilarating when failure is a distinct possibility.

Winning is really only exhilarating when failure is a distinct possibility.

Another advantage the entrepreneur has over you is that no one notices his setback, whereas you have a whole host of subordinates, peers and superiors in whose eyes you feel publicly humiliated. The entrepreneur has the challenge of rescuing his business, while your challenge is more psychological, at least initially.

Behaving entrepreneurially in a large organisation

An interesting question: can you visualise yourself as an entrepreneur while remaining a manager in a large organisation? An immediate obstacle is that you need to work with and through others. Large organisations depend more on team work than does the sole entrepreneur. So you cannot afford to slaughter your internal competitors quite so openly. There is no need for our discussion to get bogged down in the perennial debate about the virtues of individual effort versus the advantages of team work. The reality is surely that each individual and team need to work out this balance for themselves. The brute fact is that you will always strive for your own personal success but you cannot succeed if you alienate your colleagues. The key to success is to get this balance just right relative to the culture of your organisation. So lets face the fact that every manager is competing for status and influence with his colleagues no matter how loudly we beat the team work drum.

Your success is therefore dependent, just like that of the entrepreneur's, on how highly valued your services are and on how good a job you do in cultivating your key customers.

Despite your all too natural tendency to feel humiliation because of your demotion, you can nevertheless choose to react in either one of two ways:

- you can let yourself focus on what you have lost and see only the negative aspects of your demotion, or
- you can immediately try to think in terms of benefits and opportunities.

Turning setbacks into opportunities

Suppose you choose to react in the conventional way. The new Marketing Director arrives and you are in a fog of resentment, hurt and bitterness. Because you are sulking, you avoid the newcomer and treat him coldly when you cannot avoid being in his presence. William Bridges might see this as O.K. as you are supposedly in mourning. You may, of course, go even further. Whenever you get the chance, you attack his ideas (behind his back of course) and shout loudly why they won't work to anyone prepared to listen to you. Naturally, you are careful not to go too far, lest your hateful colleague complains to your mutual boss and you find yourself out the door.

What is the positive approach, then? Here, you welcome the newcomer with open arms because he does in fact have a professional marketing education and background and you are very keen to learn all you can from him. You go further here as well. You tell everyone who may be feeling sorry for you that you think this is a great move for the organisation and you extol the benefits the newcomer will bring. From the moment of his arrival, you are his closest collaborator.

Your strategy is to get close to the new Marketing Director and to be seen as offering all your support. Chances are you may be able to build on his ideas and help him to fine tune them to the peculiarities of your organisation's culture – given how much experience you have of 'how things are done around here'. As a result, your superiors start to feel that you have more to offer the marketing function than they thought. Because he is an outsider, the newcomer may well move on in a couple of years and, in the meantime, you have learned so much about marketing and contributed more to it than you ever did that you get your old position back. Alternatively, you could use your new found knowledge and joint achievements as a springboard to a similar job elsewhere, or one within a different part of your organisation.

➲ **The idea here is not to encourage disloyalty. It is rather a matter of cultivating a completely different attitude to what you might otherwise see as a personal setback.**

This approach is very entrepreneurial of you, a far cry from the advice William Bridges would give you: to acquiesce in regarding your demotion as a personal disaster and go into mourning for a suitable period.

A critical point...

This sounds like an exercise in massive self-deception you say. Now is as good a time as any to rid ourselves of an important myth. The myth is that we must change our attitude towards the newcomer *first*, then we will be able to behave differently towards him.

➲ The reality is, if not always then at least often, that *we are more likely to change our attitude by behaving differently in the first place.*

Try first, think later

So it may well be that the best advice is to behave differently towards the newcomer taking it on faith that your attitude may well fall into line. Obviously, if you are resolved to wallow in self-pity then everyone, including yourself, will see you as engaging in a pretence that is fooling nobody. Alternatively, say you elect to adopt a two-stage strategy. The first stage is to acknowledge your hurt but decide to suspend judgement until you have worked closely with the newcomer for a while. Here you have not dismissed your hurt in advance, but you have decided that you will try to learn to like the situation. This attitude at least prepares you for solid attitude change once you start behaving positively towards the newcomer. Chances are now pretty good that you will actually begin to feel positive towards the situation. In any case, you have a much greater chance of developing positive feelings this way than you would if you withdrew and spent your time sticking pins into images of your hated newcomer – or simply waited to see if your attitude might miraculously change.

Expecting change and hoping for it

While we don't expect to lose loved ones in the prime of their lives, we must continually anticipate major and unexpected role changes in our careers, perhaps several of them. A starting point in thinking differently about major personal change at work is to recognise that the intensity of your shock is a direct function of your expectations *and* how hopeful you are of them developing as you would like them to. For example, you may be surprised that the weather turned out to be foul when the forecast said it would be fair, but if you were planning to spend the day reading, it hardly matters to you. Normally, we expect *and strongly hope* that our loved ones will live out their natural lives.

➲ So, the attitude to take to the possibility of significant personal change at work is to modify *both* your hopes and expectations.

In Figure 3.1, you can see how expectations and hopes are interrelated. In *Box A*, you feel no shock or horror at all because, like the entrepreneur, you expect constant change and you are innovating in advance to keep up and to leap ahead anyway. As an entrepreneur, you may not only be hoping for change, you may be actively driving it. *Box B* reflects your unconcern about the inaccurate weather forecast when you were planning to stay indoors all day. You feel mildly surprised, but otherwise unaffected.

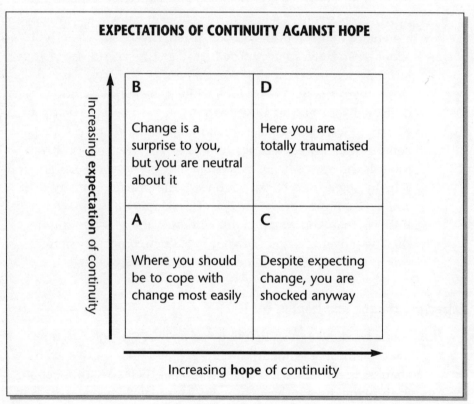

EXPECTATIONS OF CONTINUITY AGAINST HOPE

Increasing **expectation** of continuity

B

Change is a surprise to you, but you are neutral about it

D

Here you are totally traumatised

A

Where you should be to cope with change most easily

C

Despite expecting change, you are shocked anyway

Increasing **hope** of continuity

Fig 3.1

Box C is a less healthy frame of mind to be in, because here you expect change, but you are still very shocked. This shock is common to managers who expect to be made redundant: they know it will happen, the only question is how soon. But they are still shocked when it actually happens. It is the same as the death of a loved one who has been dying of cancer for months. It still comes as a shock when the person actually dies despite your expectation of the event. This is because you earnestly hope for, and depend upon, continuity in such contexts.

The account of transitions provided by William Bridges assumes that all major change in organisations falls into *Box D*. Only here does the analogy with the *unexpected* death of a loved one fully hold. You had every reason to expect your life to continue on as before and your happiness strongly revolved around your loved one. So the combination of strong expectations and strong hopes sets the stage for severe trauma. I am not suggesting that you can react any differently to the death of a loved one. The point is that, in organisations, it is only getting fired and a few other serious setbacks that are in Box D, and even these we can, in principle, regard differently with a little effort and especially if we prepare ourselves mentally to react more positively.

➲ **Most organisational changes need not be seen quite so traumatically if only managers and other employees would cultivate more positive attitudes towards change.**

Such change immunity is naturally on the increase anyway as more and more managers experience significant change as an everyday occurrence.

Figure 3.1 shows that modifying both your hopes and expectations amounts to moving yourself into Box A. Here you would take the view that change is always imminent, but you would also adopt the position that you can readily live without the status quo anyway. You might object that it is one thing to continually expect change, but why should you not at least *hope* for continuity? After all, if you have just been promoted to the position you have long had your eye on, should you not at least hope to stay in it as long as you find it desirable?

THE RISK OF STANDING STILL

What happens when you assume a very new role in an organisation? At first there is a learning curve to go through. After a while it becomes relatively routine. You may still have daily crises to cope with and significant challenges to overcome, but you are

In these days of rapid change, how long can you afford to remain in a role where you are not learning very much or very fast?

no longer learning at quite the fast rate you were when you first took over the position. In these days of rapid change, how long can you afford to remain in a role where you are not learning very much or very fast? No one is likely to admit readily to being complacent, but we all tend to consolidate our learning and to hold our ground once we get somewhere desirable, like an attractive role in the organisation. Complacency is the next step and is hard to avoid unless your role is constantly changing. While you may be working at a frantic pace and feeling anxious about the security of your tenure in this position, you still may be complacent in the sense that you are not really learning as much as you were when you were first appointed.

No doubt, this is really putting our finger on the heart of the problem:

➲ Managers have already learned to *expect* regular change, but they haven't yet begun to welcome it, to actually *hope* for change rather than hoping for continuity.

WHY to hope for change

➡ To learn continually, to keep up-to-date, to avoid stagnation.

➡ To diversify and increase your service offerings.

➡ To be able to contribute something totally new.

➡ To continue being challenged and to continue growing as a person.

➡ As soon as you are out of the firing line of intensive learning, you may start to become as complacent as an animal in a zoo.

HOW to hope for change

➡ Start thinking of a 'position' as a short-term project, not as an acquired territory that is yours to defend.

➡ Identify more with the quality of the services you can offer and less with your status in an increasingly temporary hierarchy.

➡ Recognise that your burning desire to gain and hold a position of status in a hierarchy goes back to your gorilla ancestors and convince yourself that you have moved on a bit since those days.

➡ As soon as you have worked through your learning curve, start selling yourself into a new role, move laterally if you have to, so long as you plan not to be in any one role for more than two or three years.

➡ Develop the attitude that staying longer in one role is a recipe for career and personal stagnation.

➡ Develop your staff to take over from you; prepare them and your colleagues to expect you to be around only for a short while.

➡ Focus on creating lasting value, but as if you had only two years to get everything done.

➡ Help to cultivate a culture of bearing the short-term costs of frequent movement in favour of the long-term benefits of helping employees to become more adaptable.

These points are expressed in terms of role changes, but the principle applies to how we think about any status quo situation. The idea is to expect change, but to go beyond expectations to seeing change as an opportunity to be *actively sought*, not just welcomed, much less merely agonised through *à la* William Bridges.

HOW THE ENTREPRENEUR MANAGES CHANGE

The approach to change advocated here is simply based on the age-old saying that preventing disease is better than having to cure it. This advice is not about preventing change but preventing yourself from seeing it as a tragedy. If you let yourself get into a situation where you totally expect *and* hope for continuity, you have put your eggs all in one basket so completely that you will have a tough time not being traumatised when your comfortable world collapses. This is not to say that you should go to the other extreme and never commit yourself wholeheartedly to anything.

There is no doubt that high achievers do commit themselves to a definitive line of action completely. They take risks and this means exposing themselves to very public failure. So do entrepreneurs. It's not a matter of not committing yourself, it's more about developing a new way of looking at so-called failure. Prevention in this context is about being mentally prepared to shift gears quickly rather than sinking into depression and self-pity when you suffer the inevitable setback. A lot of managers and management gurus have by now fully embraced the idea that you are not learning if you are not making mistakes.

In forward-looking, entrepreneurial, large organisations such as 3M and Asea Brown Boveri (ABB), making mistakes is seen as a sign that you are trying to innovate and that you have the guts to take risks. The safe player is now seen, not as the cleverest manager, but as something of a coward in such organisations.

⊃ **Failure is easier to take the more you fail.**

The no risk policy is the surest way to make failure seem tragic. Those who often take risks and fail are also those who succeed most often. The reward of frequent successes won at high risk is the resilience to withstand occasional failure.

So how do you shift gears this quickly, you rightly ask? It's partly about momentum: simply doing it often enough that it becomes no big deal. To shift gears quickly, you must be able to see options for yourself and have the ability to capitalise upon them. This is easy enough to see in the case of a one-person entrepreneurial business, especially in some fast-growing corner of the computer software industry. Here the very speed at which the market is changing means that there are always lots of new opportunities for someone closely in touch with how the market is developing.

We discussed earlier how the demoted Marketing and Sales Director could shift gears quickly. He may not know where his next opportunity will come from in advance of shifting gears, but by getting close to the new Marketing Director he is, in a metaphorical sense, immersing himself in his 'market' rather than withdrawing from it and licking his wounds. By getting close to the new Marketing Director, he is putting himself in a position to learn new skills, but more importantly, he will be in the best position to *watch for opportunities* as they arise. It's like if you are a lion and you fancy a zebra for lunch. You don't sit in the shade wondering where to hunt one, you go out and look around until you find one.

Deciding what to do when you don't know where you're going

The lion's approach to seeking out lunch is very much like what a few savvy managers say when they are made redundant: 'I don't know what I want to do next but I'll know it when I see it.' Through networking they put themselves in front of people in different industries and ask a range of questions that will help them decide whether this particular industry would be an interesting place to work. What they don't do is first decide by navel gazing that they will be an X in future and only then go out and find an employer of X's.

➲ **The key point here is that shifting gears in the midst of major change is not a matter of knowing in advance where next to turn, it is more a matter of beating about some likely bushes and keeping your eyes open for a good opportunity.**

You can go beyond merely keeping an eye open, of course. Getting immersed in your 'market' you may be able to be much more creative than this and see a way to combine several trends and create a new service you can offer your employer. This is the heart and soul of successful entrepreneurship.

Diversifying yourself

Realistically, a lot of employees simply cannot shift gears this quickly. If you are a 50-year-old coal miner or typewriter assembler, your options for fast adaptation are clearly more limited than those of a middle manager in a growth industry. Or you may even be a bank manager whose employer is in the midst of shutting down branches in favour of automated teller machines. No doubt these employees may require a period of mourning, as William Bridges suggests, before they can turn themselves around. Nevertheless, as redundancy counsellors will testify, there is still a wide range of attitudes that such people display when they suddenly find themselves out of work. Some see their situations as desperate, others bounce back quickly and begin analysing their transferable skills for other forms of employment. So there does appear to be an element of choice in how any employee might view such dramatic changes.

But if you believe in the value of prevention, then preparing yourself for change is a matter of managing your career more entrepreneurially no matter what you are doing at the moment. And this means continually acquiring new skills and regularly talking to people working in high-demand functions to learn where new opportunities are likely to arise. Just sitting around hoping to be the last surviving coal miner is really asking for it. What such employees need is not paternalistic pity but practical help in diversifying before it is too late.

Change that is not role-related

Suppose you are the manager of a chain of retail shops in a large diversified organisation that owns several different types of retail operations. Let's say a sister division has just successfully implemented a new computerised point-of-sale process. You don't quite see how the benefits of this innovation will justify the costs in your smaller division, but your boss insists on you proceeding with the new system anyway.

The real obstacle in this situation for you is that you are trying to see the benefits before deciding. This is the conventionally *rational* way to think, is it not? Recall what we said about changing roles where the key was precisely not to try to decide in advance what you might do next but rather first to expose yourself to some likely possibilities to see if anything strikes you as appealing.

Applying this philosophy to your chain of retail shops, you should try to get some first-hand exposure to the new process *before* deciding what to do. This will be whatever is practical for you. It might be as simple as spending a day at a shop in your sister division to see how the new system operates. Alternatively, it may be feasible for you to run a pilot project in one of your outlets to gain even more first-hand familiarity. This seems such a patently obvious way of approaching an unwelcome proposal, it seems hardly worth mentioning. But the unfortunate fact is that we are all so good at making decisions in our heads based on our own biases, prejudices, assumptions and distorted perspectives that we actually have a great deal of difficulty setting these aside and trying something unfamiliar *before* making a decision.

Backward decision making

This is like trying to decide whether you like a new, exotic type of food without first tasting it. The problem with resistance to change is that it occurs entirely in our heads. Just as you cannot learn in a new environment without experimenting and making mistakes, you cannot decide about any new change without trying it out on some basis first, however limited.

You cannot decide about any new change without trying it out on some basis first, however limited.

Because we like to think of ourselves as being so rational, we have forgotten that it is pretty hard to make decisions about matters without some direct experience of them – especially when we are saddled with some strongly opposing biases. We thus overly exalt our powers of reasoning alone to make all our decisions. Because we can react in our heads faster than we can try out something new, our mental reaction too often determines how we will behave. So the suggestion here is quite simply to suspend judgement until you have tried it. You may object: 'Why should I try it when I *know* it will not work.' While this may be true sometimes, generally this stance is a sign of poor problem-solving and decision-making processes.

Science was only able to progress during the Renaissance by people being willing to challenge comfortable assumptions. For example, as recently as the early 17th century, people still believed that heavier objects would fall to the ground faster than lighter ones because Aristotle had said so about 2000 years earlier. Galileo refuted this belief by actually dropping objects of different weights from a sufficient height simultaneously and demonstrating that they hit the ground at the same time.

Unfortunately, too many managers think they know how things will work out just because they have thought it through in their heads. What they need to do is to improve their decision-making processes by injecting a little of Galileo's experimental approach into them. Being able to review the past and rehearse for the future in our heads is a mixed evolutionary blessing. On the upside, it allows us to save time rather than having to learn everything by trial and error. On the downside, however, this rational skill can lead us to divorce ourselves too distantly from reality, hence failing to try anything because we think we know all there is to know about it already.

As we have seen, of course, it is not simply a matter of letting assumptions undermine a more experimental decision-making process. If you let yourself become too wedded to any status quo, you simply will *not want* to be proved wrong by any means in any case. This is the sort of attitude toward change that led Galileo to have to publicly recant his heretical views. He was too high-profile to burn at the stake – unlike a lot of less important heretics.

An experimental approach to making decisions is actually much more commonly used already than we care to acknowledge. We so hate to admit using anything like trial and error that, once we have reached some final decision, we hide all the blind alleys we blundered down and present the decision as having been based solely on sound reasoning. Often, the truth of the matter is that

EXAMPLE

A fairly well-known example of the trial and error approach to decision-making is how Honda came to sell small motor bikes in North America. They went to California to look into selling cars and some of the executives travelled around town on small motor bikes. The interest this aroused in bystanders, who happened to see them, led Honda to sell motor bikes. So much for rational strategic planning!

we present reasons for our decision as if we had been aware of them from the beginning when, in fact, our reasons are rationalisations contrived after the fact.

Our worship of reason divorced from experience and of planning everything we will do in advance is based on self-deception and our ability to deceive everyone else. Because we see our colleagues presenting only complete decisions and not all the trial and error they went through to get there, we feel we must make the same pretence. If you are especially good at such make believe you will even manage to fool yourself. If you are less comfortable with deception, you will feel eternally less adequate than your peers as only you seem to have to blunder into a decision while they seem able to think everything out in advance.

What has all this got to do with change?

One way of becoming more comfortable with change is to take a more experimental approach to making decisions. This means trying things out before condemning them as unworkable. At a deeper level, we are advocating killing off the *myth of reasoned decision making.*

> Managers at all levels should be encouraged to be more candid about all the blind alleys and mistakes they make before arriving at final decisions. How else are you going to have the remotest hope of encouraging employees to feel more comfortable making mistakes if you, their leaders, cannot admit your own mistakes?

Your corporate culture really needs to live and celebrate a more experimental approach to decision-making. You might even develop some ingenious slogans like 'Try before you buy!' to emphasise how serious you are about not making judgements until you have had some direct exposure to how things really work. Similarly, as change agents, the key is not about communicating the reasons for a change more fully or more clearly, the key is rather to provide people with some first-hand exposure to the new way of working on a small scale before they have to commit themselves. This does not necessarily mean involving everyone in planning or implementing the change, it just means switching from trying to *sell* the changes to letting people try them out for themselves.

> A good example of this trial and error approach is implementing a new company-wide computer system. As people are unsure of the new system, you wouldn't throw out your old system until you had worked out the bugs in the new system. It is funny, but often we say we need time to work out the bugs in a new system before we are prepared to embrace it, when this is really a face-saving way of saying that *we* need to get used to the new system ourselves before *we* can feel comfortable with it.

In more general terms, wherever it is feasible, you should maintain your old way of doing things while you try out the new approach. This makes change safer and less dramatic.

As we noted in comparing change with the death of a loved one, death is sudden and complete. Change does not need to be that dramatic if you can ease into a new way of working and simultaneously ease out of the familiar processes. This approach gives people a greater sense of control rather than having to adjust to the double shock of suddenly losing their familiar work patterns and, at the same time, having to adjust to something totally new.

CONSOLIDATING WHAT WE HAVE LEARNT SO FAR

If you look back at Figure 3.1, you will recall that the key to preparing ourselves to cope with change more effectively is to move ourselves, mentally, from Box D to Box A. This means that we need to both expect and hope for change. Change should therefore be seen as an opportunity-generating mechanism rather than as a sort of grim reaper.

→ Regardless of the type of change you are facing currently, take time to write down as many of the benefits and opportunities for you that you can see at the moment. Writing them down is much better than merely reciting them in your head as you will almost certainly generate a longer list this way. Writing down positive statements is also a known technique for convincing yourself to see things positively.

➡ Go beyond merely noting possible opportunities and benefits. Get as close as you can to the heart of the change process, resolving to gain early first-hand exposure rather than hiding in your office hoping the change will pass you by. The close view will help you to see even more benefits and opportunities for yourself. Be sure to look at the longer term if you can only see shorter-term costs for yourself. But don't expect to know what to do immediately. Stay close and keep a watchful eye out for opportunities. Talk to others as widely as you can to pick up their ideas.

➡ Cultivate a more experimental approach towards decisions about change and towards everyday decisions generally. Catch yourself making a decision and write down what assumptions you are making and ask yourself how valid are these assumptions. Check them out on a trial and error basis before committing yourself.

➡ Stop thinking that, as the manager, you need to be seen to have a ready decision at the drop of a hat for every occasion. Train your subordinates and your boss (even more importantly) to realise that only idiots make decisions at the drop of a hat in today's complex business world – insecure idiots at that.

Start thinking more like an entrepreneur.

- What is your market?
- Who are your major customers?
- Do you know their needs?
- What are your services?
- Are you innovating and developing new services?
- Do you need to start diversifying your offerings?
- Are you keeping up to date?
- Are you networking enough to keep in touch with how your market is developing and what your competitors are doing?

Most importantly, start viewing change as an opportunity for you. Going beyond this reactive mode, ask yourself what changes you can initiate that would be of benefit to you as well as to the organisation.

IT GETS HARDER AS YOU GET OLDER

Not all older people find change harder, but many certainly do. The older we get the more ancient patterns we carry around with us. Younger people are not necessarily better at change, they just have less excess baggage to unload.

Younger people are not necessarily better at change, they just have less excess baggage to unload.

In the good old days, one of the reasons we cited for wanting to become a manager was to step back from the firing line. Today, there is no escaping the firing line short of retirement. This means we have to choose, as we age, between keeping up and falling behind. You used to be able to fall behind gracefully by becoming a 'general' manager, a facilitator rather than a doer. Increasingly, however, management as a process is being built into lower and lower level jobs. Now you need to keep up with some functional skill set if you are to be seen as really adding value as you age.

The approach to managing change advocated here applies equally to older managers. They simply have to work harder to put these suggestions into practice. Their assumptions, biases, habits, hopes and expectations are more entrenched, so they will need to be more vigilant in guarding against them. As the desire and ability to stay close to the firing line wanes, the principle of behaving like an entrepreneur still applies. Only now you should be looking for liaison roles rather than general management positions.

Business is growing more complex partly because of the ever-expanding sophistication of technology. The range of products and services that could be offered is growing at the same rate. This rapid expansion means more and more specialists speaking technical languages only they can understand. How can they communicate with specialists in other fields? Professional translators, brokers and liaison experts should be very much in demand.

A corollary of seeing yourself as an entrepreneur is that you should be able to back out of the firing line gradually, working part-time as you ease yourself into new career opportunities. Retirement as a sudden transition should soon be obsolete.

We will discuss the transition to retirement in more detail later. The main point for now is that the approaches to managing change discussed here do apply to older managers even though they will no doubt have a greater struggle to put them into practice.

PRACTICAL STEPS

➡ Avoid disastrous transitions by phasing in the new and by seeing the unexpected as an opportunity.

➡ Whenever you have to face an initially unwelcome change, try to see it as an entrepreneur would see the situation.

➡ Ensure that you do your best to avoid taking any changes personally.

➡ Focus on what you will gain, not on what you are losing when some aspect of your world changes.

➡ Work at changing the way you behave before trying to change your attitude – you cannot will an attitude change but new experience can turn a negative attitude around.

➡ Try to gear yourself up to hope for change as well as expect it so that you will be more inclined to welcome change.

➡ Develop a more experimental approach to decision making, being more willing to admit to all the blind alleys you have pursued before arriving at your final decision.

SUMMARY

The key to approaching change more entrepreneurially is to let go of the defensive need to control everything. This means acting more responsively at all times and making decisions as you go. It is a myth to think that we can make complete and full decisions before taking any experimental action. Improvisation is messy and mistake-ridden, but it is how managers really make decisions so why not admit it so we can all get on, more openly, with cultivating an entrepreneurial approach to change? The flip side of a need to think everything through before acting is a hatred of surprises. But no manager can excel at change who hates surprises. Change only has to be seen as traumatic if you take it personally. In Chapter 4 we will explore why some managers get so angry in the midst of major changes and how it can get worse as we get older.

'Grief is a species of idleness.'

Samuel Johnson, Letter to Mrs. Thrale,
17 March 1773

CHAPTER

4

THE JOURNEY OF YOUR LIFE

OBJECTIVES

- To explore why it is that some managers seem to explode with anger at the slightest provocation and to look at how such anger undermines receptivity to change.

- To discuss how susceptability to anger increases with age.

INTRODUCTION

Do you recall my friend Tony from the first chapter? He was the 45-year-old engineering manager who was struggling to decide whether he really wanted to be a manager rather than a technical expert. He found himself getting increasingly angry when younger subordinates displayed some technical knowledge that he had not yet heard about. Despite running as hard as he could to keep up with his field, he saw himself slipping inexorably behind his bright young stars. What his subordinates found most baffling was the sheer intensity of Tony's anger over what seemed quite trivial issues. They saw it as reasonable that Tony might be a bit nostalgic for his younger days, but why was he *that* angry?

GETTING OLDER AND ANGRIER

In earlier chapters, we looked at the shock and anger people feel when a highly visible change is forced on them, such as a role change, for example. Such managers are settled in and happy with the status quo. But some managers just get angry at the drop of a hat, for no visible reason. Why is this? And how does it relate to coping with change?

> The short answer is that our anxiety grows as we see our time running out and this lowers our threshold for coping with the slightest provocation.

Sometimes we blow our top because we are under a lot of pressure and the last straw has just been thrown in our faces. Such outbursts of anger can be seen in younger employees – it is not restricted to those of us over 40. For all ages, outbursts can be caused by your stress threshold being lowered to the point where one extra straw becomes too much to bear. Change is not the issue at these times. But ageing brings its own stresses over and above the pressure of deadlines. Resistance to change is easily built on such foundations.

In this chapter we need to look closely at why Tony gets angry more easily as he gets older. He is not the sort of manager who just wants to drift along with the status quo, Tony has a drive to achieve something, even if he is not quite sure what. We touched briefly on the relationship between age and change in the last chapter, but much more needs to be said. Like it or not, the stereotype of the older manager being resistant to change is mostly true. Some older managers are change champions, but there is a core of truth to the generalisation, despite these exceptions to the contrary. We will also look closely at the relationship between anger, anxiety and poor adaptability more generally, for managers of all ages.

Is life a journey?

If Tony gets angry because he is anxious about running out of time, does this mean that he thinks he is going somewhere? Is he in a race and hence rightly worried about falling behind? Sometimes we fantasise about taking up a more relaxing profession so we can 'drop out of the rat race': as if we could suddenly stop worrying about running out of time once we actually started living our idealised life of leisure! The fact is that we *blame* the rat race for a feeling that we probably would have anyway. As we age we naturally start to feel anxious about time running out. This is a biological clock running down not a consequence of our particular surroundings or occupation, hectic as they may be.

When we are young we talk about career *advancement* or career *progression*, so there is a sense in which we see ourselves as being on a journey even if we don't have a highly specific destination in mind. We suppose we'll know we have arrived when we get there. Being ambitious means wanting to reach some sort of position in life. Younger people often dwell on the future: 'Everything will be great when X happens or when I become Y.'

For good or ill, we don't stop looking for better things in our future despite our advancing years. No matter how often we have 'arrived' somewhere desirable, we soon feel it's not so great after all and look ahead to something better. This can be anxiety producing in itself – the feeling of never arriving anywhere especially worthy of stopping awhile. This anxiety is then compounded by the feeling of time running out. A related frame of mind is never feeling quite ready for that big challenge, as if you have not progressed far enough along on your journey to tackle the really big jobs.

We admire people who grow old gracefully precisely because it is a rare and admirable feat. The implication is that most of us 'rage against the dying light'. Most of us feel some anxiety to get somewhere, even if we don't know where, before it's too late. If you are the sort of person who is always in a hurry and if you are frequently impatient, then you are especially susceptible to the curse of seeing yourself as never having enough time.

The positive side of this process is that there would be no progress if we were not constantly striving to better ourselves. A further requirement is to have a short memory for how well off we were in the past, thus ensuring a constant, if vague, sense of dissatisfaction with the present. Unfortunately, many of us don't seem to learn how to turn off the striving and begin to let go naturally in step with our biological clocks. So we keep pushing ourselves to get somewhere better, well past our sell-by dates. If life is anything like a journey it may perhaps be a journey up a mountain and back down the other side. Hence the reference people make after 40 to life being all downhill from here. Thinking in terms of a downhill slide from about the age of 40 also ties in with the growing, generalised anxiety we start to feel from about that age.

If life is anything like a journey it may perhaps be a journey up a mountain and back down the other side.

The frustration of having to start over

What has all this got to do with change, you ask? The longer we are in a race the harder it is to start over. If you are setting out on your summer holidays by car and five minutes down the road you realise you have forgotten something essential, it is no big deal to turn back and get it. But if you remember this item an hour or two into your journey, you just might get very angry upon realising your plight. Similarly, if you are in mid-career and change is thrust upon you, thereby forcing you to start over in some way, your anger has a comparable rationale. In Tony's case,

87

no major changes are dumped on him but he keeps seeing little signs that he is falling behind. At this stage in his journey, he sees it as too late to be losing ground, hence his blind rage.

As with your summer holiday, the further Tony gets down the road of his career, the more upset he is by the slightest of setbacks. Tony's anger shows us that some negative reactions to change really amount to disguised frustration with ourselves, with the little time we have left and the feeling that we still have not done nearly enough in the time we have used so far.

Consider again Tony's complaining about issues that seem trivial to his subordinates. How often have you heard managers, or yourself, complaining about seemingly unimportant details during a major change effort? We discussed defensiveness in an earlier chapter and this behaviour is an excellent example of counterproductive defensiveness. When Tony complains about trivia, he is really venting his anger about more substantial issues that he does not want to face.

Applying Herzberg to change

Frederick Herzberg's theory of work motivation sheds some useful light on this matter. Herzberg showed that some things, like recognition, motivate us because they are obtained when we exert ourselves to achieve something worthwhile. Other supposed motivators operate as *hygiene* factors in that giving them to us doesn't motivate us to work harder, but taking them away annoys us.

Your monthly salary is not as motivating as an earned bonus, but a reduction in your salary would certainly be *de*motivating.

A fascinating corollary of Herzberg's theory is that workers who have no motivational factors in their jobs complain loudly, but not about the lack of such factors as, say, recognition. Instead they complain about hygiene factors such as pay or working conditions.

The same workers, when well-motivated, have no problem with allegedly horrible working conditions. A good example of this is your willingness to work on your car outside in the cold and dark because you feel motivated to do it, while on the job, where you are not so motivated, you would not tolerate such poor working conditions. What is going on here? The fact is that it is too embarrassing to admit that you are unhappy on the job, that you feel no one values your work or recognises you, so you divert your anger onto something else, anything else, you can think of to complain about.

When we apply Herzberg to change, we understand more clearly that no one wants to admit feeling slighted, left out or anxious about growing older and being dumped on the scrap heap, so they complain instead about any trivia they can grasp hold of, simply to vent their rage at the injustice of life in general. Tony, after all, did not criticise his subordinates for knowing something he did not. He would have a hard enough time admitting this to himself let alone to his subordinates. Instead, he complained that their new way of doing things failed to take account of some 'critical' factor that he had learned years ago.

The moral of this story is that what you or others complain about in the face of change is not necessarily the real issue.

Change agents can easily fail at this point if they address only what you are complaining about. This would be like paying employees more just because that's what they are complaining about when the real problem may be that they do not feel really involved in their work, they get no recognition and they feel unimportant.

On the deepest level, the fear of time running out is the fear of death. If you are locked into fear mode instead of growing old gracefully, the ever-diminishing time remaining to you will only make things feel worse. Seeing younger people get ahead of you only throws it in your face.

GETTING INTO THE DRIVER'S SEAT

Part of Tony's problem is the feeling that he has no control over his life. He is aware that he has been developing a short fuse of late, but he doesn't understand why. He just feels that he is being propelled along at an ever-increasing speed to who knows where. He is not even more than dimly aware that he is getting older. Hence his surprise at seeing how old some of his friends look when he sees them after several years. Although he does his best to avoid facing the facts, the truth forces its way to the surface via his temper tantrums. Lack of time, among other reasons, has kept Tony from having a good look at who he is and what he wants out of his career and life. But it is surely only through occasional stock-taking that Tony has any hope of getting into the driver's seat and beginning to enjoy the rest of his journey.

In order to cope better with change, Tony needs to take some of the pressure off himself. Getting into the driver's seat to feel more comfortable with himself means developing a wider perspective on what is important to him. This should enable Tony to react differently to the issues that are driving him up the wall at the moment.

Tony is operating like a business with no strategy. He has drifted, out of strategic control, from one role to another with little thought of where he wants to go. As a result, he simply takes on more and more new things simply because they seem like good ideas at the time. But how can you be entrepreneurial and opportunistic if you do not grasp opportunities as they come your way? Its a question of knowing what things to think strategically about and what things to behave entrepreneurially towards.

In Figure 4.1 we can see graphically what sorts of things we should be strategic about. People on the extreme left of the horizontal axis, *Box A*, are very entrepreneurial in the sense that they immediately seize every opportunity that seems interesting at the moment. At the opposite end of this spectrum are people who cannot move without a plan, those in *Box C*. On the vertical axis, starting at the bottom, we are focusing on immediate issues while the top refers to what is of most fundamental importance to us in the broadest possible sense. Thinking strategically about your basic purpose in life does not necessarily imply a plan to get somewhere, journey metaphors aside. At this level, your strategy might simply be a set of values and beliefs about what is important to you. Like a business mission, your values at this level will guide you in your choices as you move down the scale to today's less important issues.

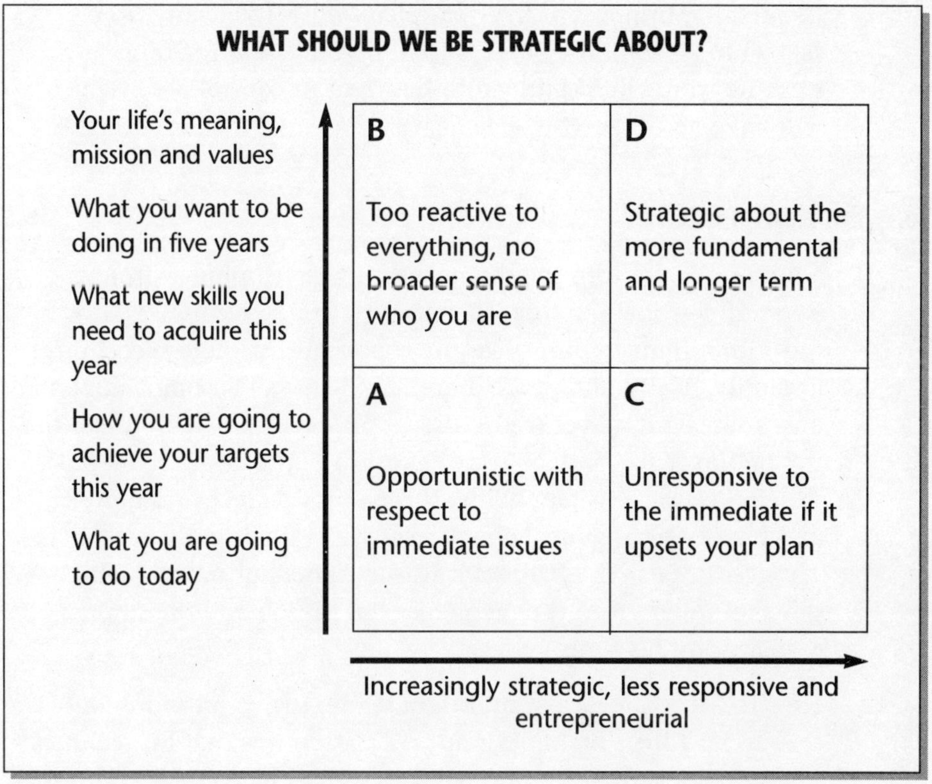

WHAT SHOULD WE BE STRATEGIC ABOUT?

Your life's meaning, mission and values

What you want to be doing in five years

What new skills you need to acquire this year

How you are going to achieve your targets this year

What you are going to do today

B Too reactive to everything, no broader sense of who you are	**D** Strategic about the more fundamental and longer term
A Opportunistic with respect to immediate issues	**C** Unresponsive to the immediate if it upsets your plan

Increasingly strategic, less responsive and entrepreneurial

Fig 4.1

Can you guess which box Tony is in? Actually he is in two boxes: A and B because he is living totally in the moment with no mission at all. Everything he does is based on immediate responsiveness. It would be just as self-defeating to be in Box C as here you would not be responsive to anything unless it happened to fit into your well worked-out plans.

➲ The ideal is to occupy *Boxes A and D* so that you are flexible and opportunistic with regard to immediate issues but guided by a broader strategy about where you are going and what is most important to you.

Your five-year plan is rightly in the mid-range. You have some idea where you would like to be but you have options and you are prepared to change direction when the time comes if it seems to fit with where you are at that moment and with your revised longer-term perspective.

Clearly, the firmness of five-year plans will vary greatly from person to person. The point is that, if you take it to Tony's extreme, you will feel driven rather than in control because you will have no underlying idea of why you are doing anything.

Tony develops a mission

Tony finally got into the driving seat by developing a stronger sense of personal purpose. He began by asking himself what was most important to him. Near the top of his list came such things as family, health and peace of mind. A sense of accomplishment and a satisfying career were close to this level but not quite at the top of Tony's list. Two of Tony's most important values needed little reflection. His family life, though not perfect, was quite O.K. and he was getting just enough exercise to maintain passable physical fitness. The harder bit was to figure out how to achieve peace of mind given the manic pace of his job and the severe demands on his time.

How to achieve peace of mind, therefore, took a lot more soul searching. Tony's first important realisation was that his technical field was splitting into sub-fields faster than he could keep up with them. He also faced the fact that his team was stronger with staff who were more knowledgeable in some areas than he could ever hope to be. So what did Tony really want for himself as far as the remainder of his career was concerned? He had always been plagued by the dilemma of whether to remain a technical specialist or to move more wholeheartedly into management.

Tony decided first of all to take the pressure off himself to be the foremost expert in all aspects of his technical field. As he became more comfortable with the fact that he was ageing, he began to see the enjoyment he got out of helping younger colleagues develop. So, he decided to strike a balance between his traditional alternatives. On the one hand, Tony decided to focus on only those aspects of his technical field that most interested him and keep up to date with them.

Tony began to think of himself as a business and he recognised the need for a personal business strategy. The implication of thinking strategically meant that he could now focus on what most interested him and what he felt he could do best rather than trying to keep up with everything indiscriminately – or unstrategically.

Tony's newly developed mission is to keep up to date with a few aspects of his field and to help develop the junior staff reporting to him. He increasingly recognises the importance of communicating technical issues more clearly across functions and he can see himself moving towards more of a liaison role as opposed to that of a technical expert.

Most importantly, Tony's soul searching helped him to take the pressure off himself. He recognised that he would prefer to grow old gracefully as this attitude would make it easier for him to make positive contributions to the organisation and to adjust to change less painfully. In turn, this new attitude enabled Tony to stop blowing his top over the slightest annoyance. In the end, Tony did achieve a better peace of mind.

What Tony learned about coping with change

Tony realised that he had coped poorly with change in recent years because he had felt in a hurry to get somewhere even though he did not know where he was going. Previously, he had seen the slightest change as a setback, a sign that he had even less time, that he was falling even further behind – hence his increasing anxiety. When he understood that his anxiety was just his reaction to the natural human ageing process and his fear of running out of time, he was able to relax, recognising that he could do nothing about it other than accept it and make the best of it. This did not mean wallowing in self-pity, but rather looking for new, more realistic opportunities.

ANGER AND RESISTANCE TO CHANGE

When strong-willed managers with high self-esteem are intensely opposed to change, they get angry. As we have seen, there may be any number of reasons for their anger. Because their self-esteem is high, they feel they have a *right* to be consulted, otherwise they feel betrayed. Of course, the more they see themselves as part of the organisation's central decision-making processes, the greater their feeling of loss, betrayal and hence anger. So this is the anger of being left out. To the extent that managers see themselves as competing with peers to control the organisation's direction, their anger will revolve around a sense of losing to the competition – as we have seen.

In Tony's case, we have looked at a new source of anger, the fear of ageing and time running out. Tony's anger was based on the fear that any change was a further sign of his fading ability to keep on top of his life.

Whatever the cause, anger is a major block to change. While it may be sound advice to see setbacks as opportunities and to react more entrepreneurially, we need to get a handle on how we can first control or minimise our angry reactions. We are not talking about mild annoyance. It is blind rage that really gets in the way and it is just as effective in killing your adaptability whether you suppress your rage or let it fly in the nearest person's face. What really gets under your skin? Try the questions in Figure 4.2.

> *Whatever the cause, anger is a major block to change.*

If you don't get enraged by any of these common annoyances, you are either very laid back or you have so successfully suppressed your anger that you don't recognise it anymore.

➦ **The most important question here is why do managers get so enraged at all?**

We looked closely at the underlying causes of Tony's rage, but getting older is one of the more reasonable excuses for blowing your top.

THE REAL REASONS FOR RAGE

If you are on a long enough holiday to fully unwind, chances are you don't find yourself breaking out in rages too frequently. So there must be some connection between the pressure of work and rage susceptibility. Some people handle pressure quite well, even

WHAT MOST ENRAGES YOU?

✔

- People making avoidable errors ☐
- Lack of effort or motivation in subordinates ☐
- Peers winning a dispute with you ☐
- Being made to look a fool ☐
- Your boss criticising you, unfairly in your view ☐
- Unexplained irrational changes imposed on you ☐
- Money seemingly wasted ☐
- Peers or subordinates knowing more than you ☐
- Making mistakes you know you could have avoided ☐
- Other departments stomping all over your territory ☐
- Being ignored or slighted by those you highly regard ☐
- Lack of attention to detail in subordinates ☐

Fig 4.2

thrive on it. There must be more to it, then. Underlying anxieties must also play a role as they clearly did in Tony's case. His underlying anxiety was the fact that he was getting older and he could feel himself inexorably slipping behind. He could cope with this anxiety on less stressful days, but when he was under pressure, his threshold for blowing his fuse was severely reduced. So Tony's continual state of anxiety, however dim and in the background, combined with work pressures caused him to lose his temper regularly. This is illustrated in Figure 4.3 overleaf.

Obviously, some people are just naturally more easygoing than others, but as Figure 4.3 shows, managers with some natural predisposition to anger can behave quite differently depending on their level of underlying anxiety. Those in *Box A* are not under a lot of work pressure and they are not particularly anxious about anything, for the most part. Other things being equal, they should

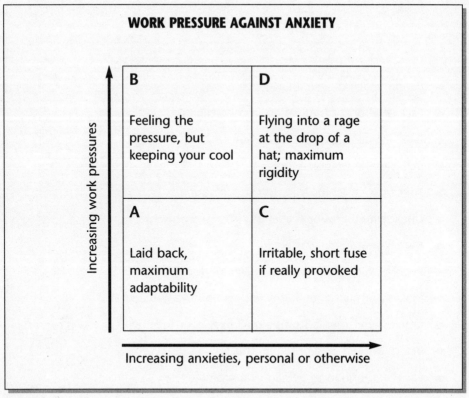

Fig 4.3

be more receptive to change than their counterparts in the other three boxes. Those in *Box B* are still relatively flexible. They are under pressure and may balk at sudden changes of priority, but they seem to thrive under pressure and they are not particularly anxious about anything, so they should be relatively adaptable as well.

Managers in *Box C* have anxieties, like Tony, even if for different reasons and they are likely to be fairly easily irritated. Getting them to change can be delicate and it very much depends on how gingerly you approach them. But as they are not under any particular work pressure, they can generally control their temper so as to avoid flying into a rage most of the time. The real problem managers are those in *Box D*. Here the combination of a steady state of anxiety and work pressures can be lethal. It is these managers whose resistance to change is most seemingly irrational.

Managers in Box D are a change agent's nightmare – walking time bombs. The cause of their outbursts of rage is not primarily the change agent's proposals, it is their own lowered anger threshold. Compare this situation with starting a fire. Suppose you throw a lighted cigarette out of your car window into wet grass. Chances are there will be no fire. However, if you throw the same cigarette into very dry grass, the chances of a blaze are much greater. In this situation, the dryness of the grass is as much a cause of the fire as your cigarette. Indeed, as compared to wet grass, the dry grass is the more important causal factor. Analogously, a manager who is fairly relaxed at work will be harder to enrage than one who is already simmering.

The moral of this story is that it is completely futile for the change agent to focus exclusively on how he approaches the simmering manager – it will only take the proverbial last straw to break the camel's back anyway.

➲ **The key to improving the receptivity to change of such managers, or yourself if you are the simmering one, is to find ways to dampen down anger thresholds more generally.**

Compare this to the fire analogy. If the grass is dry, there is unlikely to be any way you can toss your lighted cigarette out the window safely, no matter how carefully you throw it. If you could order up some rain to wet the grass first, then you might get away with no fire. Fortunately, it is not quite as impossible to cool down simmering managers as it is to conjure up a downpour.

Why are you getting more short-fused?

We need to understand why managers are simmering in the first place before we can figure out how to help them turn down the heat. Remember Herzberg applied to change? We found that people may often complain about trivia as a way to unload their anger at the injustice of life in general. The injustice of life for Tony was his dim awareness of slipping behind, of running out of time as he aged. Rather than embarrass themselves by admitting their real fears and anxieties, managers just simmer because of these fears and anxieties until someone throws that

Rather than embarrass themselves by admitting their real fears and anxieties, managers just simmer.

97

lighted cigarette in their direction and sets them ablaze. If they are simmering enough, it won't take much of a spark to ignite them.

Did you tick any of the supposed causes of rage in Figure 4.2? Most of these 'causes' will only really get under your skin if you are already about to explode.

Causes of short-fusedness

If you have a short fuse, it may be because...

- you see yourself as losing, or at least not winning
- you do not feel accepted or valued
- you fear not being competent enough to deliver
- you feel you do not have enough resources or time
- your job does not stimulate you
- you have one or two personal problems
- you are the sort of person who is generally tense.

What has all this got to do with change? Well, if you disturb a simmering manager, he will boil over. Any change is likely to be just the disturbance it takes and an excessively angry manager is not a very flexible one.

Let's look at each of these causes of short–fusedness in turn.

1. The feeling of losing – or at least not winning

Tony felt he was losing a lot – losing his touch, losing ground in the race to stay ahead, losing his confidence, losing his youth. You may have lost something more concrete recently, perhaps a promotion you had your heart set on. Or, like Tony, you may just feel a vague sense of not getting ahead fast enough, hence not winning as easily as you used to. You may be losing political battles more regularly of late. Perhaps, as a result, you are not quite so much in the limelight this year as you were last. You may be losing territory – your patch may have been carved up, leaving you with less turf than you once controlled.

If you are feeling a generalised, ongoing state of anger due to some such loss, you are definitely not likely to complain to your boss or colleagues about the real issue. How many managers would say to their boss, 'Look, don't I count for anything around here anymore?' Whiners don't get ahead in macho cultures. You need to be tough and resilient to be a survivor. So what do you do: you simmer and blow up at the drop of a hat. Any minor provocation will do.

You are like a business that once had the market-leading product but which is now losing market share. As we discussed earlier, you can choose to react to your loss in one of two ways:

- You can go into a state of mourning as Bill Bridges might advise you to do. (A related state is just to sulk and feel angry as Tony was doing.)

- Or, you can think of yourself as an entrepreneur and take a closer look at how your internal market is developing. Then do an audit of your offerings and start innovating to get yourself back into the centre of things. This is not a matter of toughing it out macho-style or of whining. The key is simply to behave entrepreneurially, to improvise and to bounce back as quickly as you can.

Organisations are political entities and very much a world unto themselves. As a complex social environment, in which you are competing with others for personal success, it can be very difficult to avoid being too internally focused. Organisational politics can be distracting, making it that much more difficult to focus externally. If you lose a political battle, your focus will again be directly on your internal enemies. Anger directed inwards undermines receptivity to change.

Anger directed inwards undermines receptivity to change.

➲ **To regain influence, you need to behave like a leader. This means leading the way to noteworthy achievement in improving your organisation's competitive advantage relative to external competitors – your real enemies.**

Significant achievement will raise your self-esteem and, if you feel good about yourself, you will be more receptive to change.

2. You do not feel accepted or valued

You may have experienced this feeling when someone new joins your group and seems to be getting more attention than you used to get. They are now more involved in important decisions and you seem to be relegated to the periphery of the action. Or, it may be a long-standing colleague who just came up with some innovative product or performance improvement ideas and he is suddenly in the limelight that you used to occupy. This feeling also clearly involves loss. But the feeling of not being valued does not depend on losing any status you once held. You may have never been as central to your team's core decision-making processes as you would like, only perhaps you never noticed it. You have just been simmering for years without realising why.

If you feel less valued than you think you should be, chances are you feel a vague sense of resentment. In this state of mind, when someone suggests implementing a significant change, your first response may be to see this as a chance to get your revenge. You will be especially likely to want to get even if the change proposer is your enemy – the villain who you see as hogging the limelight undeservedly. You may not see your objections to the proposed change as based on a desire for revenge. To you, your objections will be sound, rational reasons why the suggested new way of doing things cannot work. You won't realise that you were predisposed to be antagonistic in the first place or that your predisposition is actually preventing you from seeing the very real benefits of the change.

It is only through being aware of the real reasons for your anger and resentment that you have any hope of being able to rise above them. It will take a good deal of courage, however, to admit even to yourself that it is not your 'enemy's' ideas that you think are stupid. It is your own jealousy for not being so highly sought after yourself that is fuelling your anger and resentment. Because you are letting these negative emotions govern your life, you are undermining your own ability to adapt to change, hence hurting yourself more than your 'enemy'.

So, what can you do about it?

➡ The first step is to analyse your own emotional reactions as honestly as you can. Try then to set your negative feelings aside. It may help you to make a list of the positive qualities possessed by the target of your resentment or of the change initiative itself. Try also to separate out what *you* think is right from what might be in the organisation's best interest.

➡ A second step is to get clear about what others do value about you. What contribution are you making that others value? Just because you are not valued for the same skills that others bring to the party, that doesn't mean you are not equally valued for other skills. Can you ascertain what these skills are? What it is that people value about your contributions? If you are feeling particularly unvalued, you need to watch that your self-esteem is not so low that you cannot see how you add any value at all. If you feel this way, it is almost certainly a figment of your own imagination. Otherwise, who would employ you?

➡ A third step is to behave more entrepreneurially as we discussed above. Move yourself closer to the centre of the action instead of sitting and sulking on the periphery. Get yourself involved in key dialogues with a range of stakeholders until you find yourself making a more central contribution. Your attitude generally will then be more positive and your anger threshold will drop, making you more receptive to change.

3. You do not feel competent enough to deliver

This is a big one. The pressure of business is rising, due primarily to increasing complexity, faster pace and the need to do more with less. You are being given more responsibility more quickly and your results are much more visible than they ever were in the past. Your anxiety about failing is also about as high as you can manage to control it. You are really simmering in this state of mind. Any added pressures, minor provocations or unexpected changes thrust in your face, may just cause you to boil over.

Your resistance to change is due to your feeling that you are already stretched to the limit and need just a thread of stability to keep you from dropping all the balls you are juggling. Your

101

anxiety is likely to be felt more as fear than anger or resentment, but the effect is the same: any added provocation and you go past the simmering stage.

This is not just a feeling of not having enough time. You actually question your ability to deliver. Under today's business pressures, the risk of failure is indeed higher.

To improve your receptiveness to change in this state of mind, you need first to change the way you look at your situation. Let's assume that you cannot negotiate new deadlines, get more resources, delegate more or take any of the standard ways out. Your only option, therefore, is to view your predicament differently.

Part of viewing the situation differently is, of course, to view your own competence more positively. The short answer here is that you are probably as good as anyone to manage this project. Your chances of success are likely no worse, even if no better, than any your peers would have if they were in your shoes.

➲ **A good practical step to take is to get regular feedback on how others think things are going.**

Getting feedback ties in with keeping others in the picture. Keep major stakeholders fully up to date with the state of your project, all of the constraints and risks associated with it. This is just good communication and project management, not whining. At the same time, it is important not to go overboard in this direction, dwelling excessively on all the reasons why your project might fail.

Psychologists have discovered a phenomenon they call 'self-handicapping'. Essentially, people who fear failure may handicap themselves in some way to ensure that they do indeed fail. They will pick some publicly acceptable handicap so they will have a face-saving excuse when they fail. This gets them off the hook because failure cannot then lead to questions about their competence.

EXAMPLE

You might fire a key team member for some cooked up reason so that you can then blame the failure of the project on the loss of this person at a crucial time.

> **Self-handicapping is just a modification of the usual face-saving strategies.**

Or you might antagonise a supplier or colleague so their hostility can then be blamed for any delays to your project.

This may sound far-fetched, but we all excel in finding excuses after the fact for our failures – anything but admit a gap in our own competence. Self-handicapping is just a modification of the usual face-saving strategies.

To avoid sinking to this level of escapism, the first step is to recognise that your anxiety level is dangerously high and that you have no leeway to cope with any unexpected annoyances or changes. Anxiety is often global and nebulous. The best remedy for global feelings is to write down your concrete concerns, the specific issues that are most bothering you. Making them concrete will make action plans to counter them easier to see.

4. The feeling that you do not have enough resources or time

Here you see yourself as fully competent to do the job but you feel that everyone's expectations are totally unrealistic. In this situation, you are likely to feel anger rather than fear – or a mixture of the two. It is quite often the case that those who ask you to do something have not thought it through fully enough to appreciate how much work is involved. You are not helping yourself if you whine, sulk or simmer with anger. The key is to avoid getting yourself into overload mode in the first place by managing your stakeholders' expectations. If you have agreed up front that you will deliver, then it is always hard to go back and start hedging. So you need to be sure you agree a review process in advance so that your stakeholders *expect* you to revisit terms and conditions at various stages and to re-negotiate priorities as needed. If they expect you to be re-negotiating periodically, then, when you do, they cannot see it as you reneging on a commitment.

A further point is to be sure, as far as possible, that you ask for time to assess the resource requirements for any project before committing yourself in the first place. But even when you do take this step, there is still nothing wrong with building in a revisiting process so your stakeholders see it as normal rather than as a cause for concern.

5. Your job does not stimulate you

If you feel bored with your job, chances are you also feel a vague sense of resentment, frustration or anger. You will feel like just putting in time. Saddled with this state of mind, you will be very unreceptive to requests to alter your routines. This is because having to do the job at all will be sufficiently annoying that any requests to put out additional effort will be the proverbial last straw for you. Such boredom can often be accompanied by a loss of self-esteem, a feeling of worthlessness that can lead to a vicious circle. In this state of mind, you may feel you have no control over the situation. It is hard to have low self-esteem and, at the same time, feel that you can do something about your situation, hence even lower self-esteem – a vicious circle again.

The key here is awareness of the real causes of your feelings. Boredom is no reflection on your ability. We all need a mixture of ability *and* opportunity if we are to both excel and feel good about ourselves. The answer to your predicament, therefore, is to find a better opportunity. If you are thinking like an entrepreneur, as it has been suggested many times in this book, then you should mix more closely with parts of the organisation where opportunities might lie. Sitting and waiting for your guardian angel to pluck you out of your miserable job will get you nowhere.

6. Personal problems?

Clearly, if you have personal problems, on top of a heavy workload, you will not be receptive to any added pressures whether unexpected changes, things going wrong or simply added work. The important point here is that you should not soldier on as if nothing was the matter. If your boss really does value your services, he should be willing, for a short time, to make allowances on your various deadlines or to re-negotiate some of your priorities. Not talking about it is a recipe for short-fusedness and negative reactions to change.

➲ **Again the idea is to manage the expectations of key stakeholders. If they expect you to function as normal, then you are in for trouble if you fail to meet those expectations. However, if you keep your main stakeholders in the picture, they can prepare themselves accordingly until you sort out your personal issues.**

7. Always feel a bit uptight and tense?

Some people react angrily to change simply because their stress threshold is always low. It is not a matter of temporarily feeling work-related anger, anxiety or fear. Nor is it anything to do with personal problems. Some people are just biologically wired to be provoked into flying off the handle more readily than others. If this is your situation, you may be able to recognise it by noticing that you have nearly always been uptight, tense and easily angered, even as a child or teenager at school. Have you always had to make an effort to be cheerful? Have you always had to fake a smile? Do you frown when others are taking time out for a laugh? Are you the perennially serious sort? If so, then you will not be as receptive to change as you could be. To enhance your adaptability, you will be doing yourself a favour if you can learn to relax and have more fun at work. A course on stress management may help, along with some personal counselling.

KEEPING ANGER AT BAY

Adaptability depends on several factors. In this chapter we have been discussing the importance of having an enthusiastic, forward-looking and positive attitude instead of living in a state of continual anger, resentment, fear or anxiety at work. Being positive is equated with being entrepreneurial in the work environment because the entrepreneur is someone who sees setbacks as opportunities and who capitalises on them to move forward rather than, self-defeatingly, reacting with anger. A positive attitude means always looking at setbacks to determine the benefits, the upside and the opportunities that can work to your advantage.

Being positive is also about being realistic with respect to the pressures you put on yourself so that you are not too devastated by seeming failure. It is especially critical to be vigilant about the emotional bases of most of your reactions to change, to realise that the objections it is so easy to raise are often emotional rationalisations that you are using because of some deeper frustration.

Hillsborough College

Learning Resource Centre
Telephone 0114 2602254

➲ It will take courage, as well as vigilance, to recognise and acknowledge your own irrationality, not to mention managing it successfully.

PRACTICAL STEPS

➡ Convince yourself to age gracefully and not go kicking and screaming.

➡ Whenever you feel angry, take time to write down the most obvious reasons for your anger, then force yourself to analyse what deeper frustrations made you short-fused in the first place.

➡ Find someone patient to talk to about your underlying frustrations.

➡ When change is initiated by colleagues you do not like, work hard to note down on paper all the positive benefits of the proposed change.

➡ When you are asked to take on a major new project that is not at all straightforward, be sure to negotiate some form of revisiting process, so you can re-negotiate priorities without seeming to be failing.

➡ Whenever you suffer a setback or lose some ground for whatever reason, try to ask yourself what a true entrepreneur would do in this situation.

SUMMARY

No manager who is constantly simmering with rage just below the surface can adapt readily to change. Unless you are naturally tense, your rage is likely to be due to some felt injustice: getting older is not fair, especially as you see yourself losing ground to younger people. To avoid becoming a victim of the downward spiral of increasing rage, you need to first recognise your own emotional state and what is causing it. Then you need to address your unique causal factors one by one in order to find a more relaxed state to live in. This may involve viewing yourself and your life quite differently. No easy task but essential if you really want to be a change champion and not a grumpy party pooper.

So far we have been discussing resistance to imposed change. In Chapter 5 we turn to the problem of breaking bad habits, where even though you may be keen on change, you can't sustain the effort despite the best will in the world.

'Custom, then, is the great guide of human life.'

David Hume, *Enquiry Concerning Human Understanding*

BATTLING INERTIA – BREAKING BAD HABITS

OBJECTIVE

- To find ways of sustaining the well-intentioned effort to break bad habits and to overcome organisational inertia.

INTRODUCTION

Thus far we have discussed explicit resistance to change, the unwillingness or inability of some managers to accept the need for change. But one of the most formidable obstacles to change is simply inertia – personal and organisational – despite the best intentions of managers who start out as change enthusiasts.

You have all seen it happen – a bandwagon gets rolling to initiate some allegedly life-saving organisational change, only to see it disappear into oblivion months later. Pressure to attend to more 'important' business takes over and you are back where you started – if you even got off the ground in the first place.

In this chapter we need to take a close look at the causes and possible remedies of personal and organisational inertia. Let's see what we can do about changing personal habits first – while recognising that personal bad habits in an organisational context may not change unless the culture changes too.

THE INERTIA OF HABIT AND THE HABIT OF INERTIA

Your New Year's resolutions

How many personal habits did you resolve to change this year? Pick your New Year's resolutions from the following list – or add your own:

- read more, learn more about X
- spend more time coaching subordinates
- network more widely
- spend more time with customers
- relax more, get uptight less easily
- smoke/drink/eat less
- get more organised, more in control of time
- become more assertive
- spend more time with the family, travel less

- delegate/empower more
- become more creative, innovative, entrepreneurial
- manage by walking around more
- develop a more strategic/visionary perspective
- streamline some major processes
- stop venting frustrations so aggressively.

If you sincerely want to do any of these things, why is it so hard? If you want to travel to an exotic vacation spot as badly as you want to change a bad habit, why is planning a trip so easy by comparison?

As a rational person, you make the most logical decisions of earth-moving significance every day without the slightest difficulty. Applying your finely tuned logic to a bad habit, you decide to change it. Same decision-making process, apparently, but the habit refuses to go away. Are you not as rational as you thought, perhaps? Are you really so weak-willed, you ask yourself?

What are some of the obstacles you find blocking your ability to change a bad habit?

- It takes too much time and effort.
- I really need to do things in my old way sometimes.
- Under pressure, I naturally fall back into my rut.
- My habits are comforting and satisfying, changing them is stressful.
- Everyone around me is doing the same old things.
- My organisation, family and friends reward my old habits.
- I don't experience any immediate payoff with the new behaviours.

How your bad habits make you feel good

There is no doubt about it, changing a bad habit does take enormous effort and a lot of time. For whatever reason, we get some form of immediate gratification out of our habits. Smoking, drinking and eating excessively does relieve stress. Shouting at someone gets the frustration out of our system. Work pressures make us react immediately and take on too much extra work, destroying our best efforts to be more organised and in better control of our time. When the boss confronts us with an urgent need, our resolve to be more assertive and tell him we are too busy disappears. And, of course, so many good ideas just get pushed onto the back burner for lack of time because of more urgent or important priorities.

There is an important truth in the realisation that our bad habits are sustained by immediate gratification of some sort – there generally is no similarly instant reward for doing the opposite. For example, if smoking relieves your stress, what happens to your stress if you don't smoke? You remain uptight, an unpleasant feeling you really need to get off your back. Even being disorganised can bring some immediate gratification. By reacting to every fire that comes your way, you gain a sense of instant achievement. It's like you are drowning. Frantically treading water at least keeps your head above water.

What all habits have in common, therefore, is their dogged perseverance thanks to some form of immediate reward. They satisfy a need even though we may not always recognise what that need might be. It is simple enough to recognise how smoking or yelling at someone immediately makes us feel

Avoiding a negative situation is its own reward.

better, but what about a more work-related bad habit like not delegating enough, for example? What is it about not delegating that can make us feel good? Perhaps you like to ensure that certain things are done properly. Maybe you feel good doing something that is no effort for you: something you are especially good at.

When you feel the slight but nagging anxiety that leads a smoker to reach for a cigarette, keeping busy can alleviate the feeling. Taking care of tasks that are routine for you creates a feeling of busyness that allows you to forget the harder jobs that force you to sit – less actively – and just think what to do. Just sitting and thinking about harder, more strategic issues is precisely when anxiety creeps up on you, like the water flooding into your lifeboat when you stop bailing for a minute.

Perhaps you do not delegate because your boss expects you to
have ready answers to his detailed questions. So you immerse
yourself in detail to avoid your boss's wrath. Avoiding a negative
situation is its own reward. In any case, you feel good precisely by
maintaining your bad habit.

Instant rewards piled on immediate pressures

We have concluded that bad habits are sustained by some sort of
feel-good factor. They also have in common a focus on the short
term, on doing something that alleviates an immediate pressure.
While we can make a long-term plan to take a vacation next year at
some exotic resort, it is surprising how much we are governed on a
day-to-day basis at work by immediate demands and pressures. You
can see how this operates for you when you return to work after a
lengthy holiday or even after the weekend. It takes you a while to
get up to speed, because you wound down to a large extent on your
holiday. It is not a question of simply willing yourself to get back up
to speed when you return to work. It is the actual, daily demands
you have to face that wind you back up again, until you reach your
normal momentum. You don't have the same buzz on holiday
because those demands have been left behind.

The fact of the matter is that we are more controlled by immediate
pressures and demands coming at us from all directions than we care
to admit, given our exalted opinion of ourselves as the supremely
rational animal. Immediate pressures force us to do what has always
worked best for us under pressure in the past, hence shoving good
intentions to use more productive habits into the background.

So, the combination of:

● being enslaved to what is happening in our immediate
environment, and

● the good feelings we get by deploying our favoured shortcuts

keep us in the stranglehold of bad habits.

Making war on your bad habits

Thus far we have identified two major reasons why it is so hard to
break bad habits:

- they make us feel good, and

- pressure makes us take shortcuts.

There is at least one other crucial disincentive to stick with a new habit:

➡ **we tend to keep our resolutions to ourselves.**

By not telling anyone of our plans to change, we are making it as easy as possible for ourselves to abandon our good intentions the moment it becomes inconvenient to sustain the effort. Or we just tell our spouse or best friend. Because a good friend understands and forgives our lapses, this is as good as telling no one.

The key to breaking a bad habit – and I'm not saying it's easy – is to set up a tough, rigorous system of substitute behaviours, rewards and punishments. You need to find your old habit more punishing to sustain than you do now and find your new habit, despite the greater effort associated with it, more rewarding.

Take delegation again as a convenient example. Suppose you have resolved to delegate more of the tasks you would typically attend to yourself. Your personal change plan should be made up of the following steps:

➡ **The first thing to do is to define as precisely as possible what 'more delegation' means. You may not be able to establish easily how many things you are delegating now each week that you would not normally delegate, but let's say it is none. The important thing is to be as precise as you can be about what you are measuring. Your subordinates should be recruited to monitor whether you are really delegating tasks that you would normally do yourself.**

➡ **Publicise your change plan as widely as you can. You have already enlisted your subordinates. Ask your boss to hold you accountable in your annual performance appraisal as well. Further, pick a colleague with whom you have a friendly rivalry. Have a competition with him, assuming he has a habit he would like to change as well. The competition would be easier to monitor if you both had the same habit to change. Pick a time frame of at least six months, or better one year, with the loser having to pay a sizable penalty.**

➡ **Publicly monitor your successes on a weekly basis. This means putting a chart on a highly visible wall to be filled in by your subordinates. They will record each instance of your delegating a task that you would normally do yourself.**

➡ **Ensure that you are punished for lapses into your old habit by having your subordinates give you minus points for doing a task that they think you could have delegated.**

➡ **Schedule regular reviews of your progress. If you hold monthly meetings, put your change effort on the agenda as a regular item. This forces you to discuss how you are doing monthly. If you do not do this, you and your subordinates will get busy and your publicly displayed progress chart will not be kept up-to-date.**

Of course this is a highly contrived solution, but nothing less intensive will work. (And, obviously, there is no guarantee that this will either.) Bad habits have too strong a hold on us and they are fed very sustaining food to keep them in place. No *ad hoc* approach or sheer effort of will can take the place of a fully structured plan with clear, public rewards and punishments.

HOW THE ORGANISATION WORKS AGAINST YOU

Delegation was an easy example to discuss because no one is involved but you and, to a lesser extent, your subordinates. The broader organisation has less to do with it. Only two things are working against you:

● the feel-good factor that sustains your inclination not to delegate, and

● the pressure to succumb to short-termism.

Suppose you resolve to change a habit that requires much more co-operation from the organisation at large. Let's say your organisation has been preaching greater team work for the past two years but with little progress to date. You recognise that you could be a better team player yourself so you decide to see what you can do to set an example for your peers, superiors and subordinates.

So, you go out of your way to help peers. You give ground more often on turf issues for the greater good of the organisation and you see that the teams you are on get rewarded as teams, not as assemblies of individuals. But at the end of the year, it is obvious to you that individual stars are getting all the glory and, in fact, you are penalised for not meeting all your targets. You missed a few of your targets because of sacrifices you made in the interest of team work. So now what happens to your resolve to be a better team player? Out the window!

It is an all too common complaint: 'If only this place could be more consistent! They preach one thing and do the opposite'. Some organisations are certainly far too inconsistent, but to keep things in perspective, we have to note that inconsistency is an essential feature of successful businesses and that will not change.

> *The type of inconsistency that causes problems is committing yourself to one thing, then doing the opposite.*

The virtue of inconsistency

Organisations are laden with contradictions to the core:

- Team work is absolutely essential but so are leaders – individuals. You need to encourage team work while simultaneously identifying leaders and encouraging them to develop.

- Managers need to keep costs down, but at the same time invest in developing new products and services.

- You need to renew the organisation for long-term survival, but keep your eye on the bottom line to make short-term profit as well.

- Organisations need to be more entrepreneurial, creative, fluid, but also efficient, if they are to be profitable – this means rule-bound and process driven

- There must be an agreed vision and single-minded direction, but not conformity and blind followership. Diversity and conflict are just as critical, if myopia and inflexibility are to be avoided.

- Open communication is essential, but being destructively direct is counterproductive.

117

● A simple message or vision is necessary for maximum clarity, but one's plan of action also has to be as complex as the task at hand.

This list could be extended indefinitely. Managing has always been a balancing act, so the sorts of 'inconsistencies' listed above are not necessarily negative. The type of inconsistency that causes problems is committing yourself to one thing, then doing the opposite. Organisations are all too good at this type of inconsistency as well.

Organisational support for a change

If we consider again the example of your endeavour to be a better team player, the problem here is that your organisation may not have made it perfectly clear what is to be understood specifically by team work and how the importance of rewarding teams is to be balanced against the need to encourage individual leadership. Your senior executives want more team work but they stop at exhortation. This is about as effective as you exhorting yourself to delegate more rather than taking the extensive steps we discussed above.

If your business is serious about team work, there must be no confusion about what exactly this means and how it will be rewarded relative to individual effort. Perceived inequity and negative inconsistency will kill the motivation to change much more quickly than will mere individual inertia alone.

Organisational rigor mortis sets in when some people are trying to change while others drag their feet.

So what is the cause of organisational inertia – as opposed to individual inertia? Organisational rigor mortis sets in when some people are trying to change while others drag their feet. Or when your business leaders are preaching one thing while setting the opposite example. Or when a change initiative that everyone is enthusiastic about is slowly put to death by short-term pressures to do the opposite, to revert back to organisational bad habits.

No doubt you can think of all sorts of ways in which your organisation fails to support your efforts to change. For example, how often have you heard senior executives bemoaning the lack of honest upward communication, on the one hand, while welcoming only good news, on the other hand. How many such counterproductive inconsistencies can you think of?

Overcoming organisational inertia

The way to undo the inertia in your organisation must surely be the same one you use to break your own bad habits. The key is to move beyond exhortations to a highly explicit definition of the new behaviours you want to see across the organisation, specify how you will measure them and how they will be monitored and rewarded. The more public and visible the process, the greater the likelihood of successful change.

⊃ **One of the surest ways to fuel organisational inertia is to let short-term pressures push aside longer-term change efforts.**

Not that you should not put a fire out if one starts or ignore an urgent crisis. This is why managers need a very public scorecard with regular progress feedback, even if done by anonymous questionnaire. The commitment to change must be as public as possible with explicit and significant consequences built in to prevent backsliding. Rewards and punishments must be delivered to all who deserve them.

Beware the conformity trap

As much as it is reasonable to do so, you must expect every department, function or division within your business to live by the new rules. At the same time, don't forget our virtuous inconsistencies. This means being crystal clear about what you will allow to be legitimate exceptions. For example, one popular change agenda today is to make large organisations more entrepreneurial. But does this mean every part of your business needs to be equally entrepreneurial? Or, if so, that being entrepreneurial must mean the same thing in every area of your business? Surely not.

All businesses need to get the balance right between delivering today's offerings efficiently and hence profitably, while at the same time creating tomorrow's offerings entrepreneurially. These are diametrically opposed functions. Either each manager needs to wear two hats – an entrepreneurial hat and an efficiency one – or different departments need to specialise. Either way, someone needs to enforce efficient, invariable processes for cost minimisation and profit maximisation while someone else needs to be more responsive, spontaneous and less rule bound. Some of your staff may need to wear one hat one day and the other the next – just as you need to be a team member in one team and a leader in another.

To avoid chaos in living with these confusing inconsistencies, it is clearly vital to define what it means to be entrepreneurial in behavioural terms and who needs to exhibit these behaviours in what situations. Such clarity will tell you which managers need to be more entrepreneurial and which need to major on efficiency. If you do not get this balance right and make it crystal clear who is to behave in what way, managers will perceive only negative inconsistency and that will kill their motivation to change, hence the usual onset of organisational inertia.

➲ **The point of this line of reasoning is that it is a mistake to expect everyone to follow the same line in an organisation. Not everyone needs to be a team player in the same sense just as not every manager needs to be entrepreneurial.**

If you expect uniformity that's what you'll get – not a dynamic, creative culture. So when you start explicitly defining the change-related behaviours you want, be sure not to go overboard in the name of consistency when some functions clearly need to behave differently.

The desire for consistency, if excessive, is itself one of the great unseen obstacles to change. Consistency is reassuring to people under pressure and top executives often need too much of it simply to feel on top of things. While there is virtue in a top executive keeping the message simple, hence clear, too much simplicity ignores real complexities across the organisation. Just as we are hearing management gurus claim that your internal organisation needs somehow to match the complexity of your environment, so it is true that your approach to creating an adaptive culture needs to take account of the real complexity within your organisation.

HOW ORGANISATIONS CAN PROMOTE A CHANGE MINDSET

What are some of the other ways in which organisations can support and foster change? We have discussed the value of constructing new reward systems based on explicit behavioural expectations and a highly public monitoring process.

Change can only be encouraged by explicitly rewarding the behaviours you want to nourish. But these need not be restricted to particular change initiatives such as the organisation's desire to be more entrepreneurial. Managers can also be rewarded through your performance appraisal process for the number of changes they initiate on a regular basis, for the number of new skills they have learned and for the assistance they have provided to help others change.

Let's look in a bit more detail at how organisations can encourage managers to be more adaptable and responsive to change. There are several steps you can take.

1. Stamp out organisational defensiveness

Let's say you just acquired a demanding new Chief Executive who you are keen to impress. To make a positive impact on him you want to be seen doing the sorts of things he will admire and not what he might regard as a total waste of time. This is a recipe for covering your tracks just in case you make an otherwise fatal mistake. But if everyone is falling over themselves trying to make the right impression, who is going to take any risks? You might go along with proposed changes simply in order to be seen by your new boss as a 'team player', but will you really initiate any change – unless you have proceeded cautiously enough to get it rubber stamped?

The closer you get to the top of the organisational pyramid, even in today's flattened pyramids, the more visible are your mistakes. The pressure of business competition puts an almost excessive premium on getting things right, of excelling and of being seen to make outstanding contributions. Failure is terrifyingly visible and so humiliating. Because you have excelled in order to get where

121

you are, you have a reputation to uphold. It is your reputation, more than the organisation's competitiveness, that you fear damaging by a silly error. You remember what it was like when you were kids – when you were ridiculed if you said something really stupid. You would almost like to say nothing out of the ordinary to avoid that ridicule.

In your visible position in the organisational hierarchy, you have not only your peers' ridicule to fear but the power your superiors have over you. In today's revolving door executive suites, you could be gone tomorrow if you don't maintain yesterday's star status performance. In this context, any risk automatically becomes high-risk. If your judgement is ever questioned, when you have this mindset, what else are you likely to do but defend yourself?

Defensiveness is only necessary because the penalty for seeming to be in the wrong is too great. A macho culture forces everyone to be strong and this usually means that it is too humiliating to make mistakes. Overcoming defensiveness requires being aware of it as a first step. The next step is to celebrate the opposite – openness about mistakes. Defensiveness will only evaporate once the fear of error has fled.

2. Celebrate risk taking and experimental decision making

We advocated earlier the need for organisations to celebrate a more experimental approach to decision making. The idea here was for everyone to admit openly the blind alleys they pursued before arriving at the correct decision rather than presenting a final decision as if you had reasoned it through with no trial and error messy blunders. Undoing organisational defensiveness includes this idea and extends it to suggesting a far more open communication culture in general, one in which all managers thank each other for bad news rather than shooting the messenger.

Immediately, however, we run up against one of our virtuous inconsistencies.

➲ **While all managers need to be more open about the mistakes they make, there is no question that some managers, by the nature of their roles, must make far fewer mistakes than others.**

Every organisation must deliver today's offerings profitably and this means high quality and low cost. In turn, achieving these attributes entails minimising errors. Hence, the 'right first time slogan'. At the same time, in order to keep up with changing markets, the same organisation needs simultaneously to be fluid, dynamic, innovative, entrepreneurial and risk orientated. How can you be all these at the same time, you rightly object?

The suggestion here does not require any individual manager to be schizophrenic, even if the organisation as a whole might seem as though it doesn't know whether it is coming or going. Individual managers either have to specialise in the 'delivery' side of your operations, while others major on organisational 'renewal', or each manager has to take on some of each aspect at different times in different contexts.

The moral of this story is that however much some parts of the organisation need to be efficient and mistake-free, other parts need to do the opposite and celebrate risk taking.

Why is this so hard to do? The problem is that many organisations have over emphasised efficiency, not because of the rational need to deliver quality products at low cost but rather because of an irrational need on the part of some senior executives to be in control. As we saw earlier in discussing the need for consistency, being out of control can be anxiety producing and if you are a senior executive whose job is always on the line, you could find it very difficult to let go, to avoid wanting to control everything to make absolutely certain no disaster befalls your patch while you are in charge. Like most anxiety-based behaviours, this one too is severely self-defeating. However much you may succeed in keeping things on the rails in the short term, your controlling style is a recipe for disaster in the long-term, innovation, renewal, entrepreneurship front.

To succeed in today's fast-changing business world, you need to get the balance right between efficient delivery of today's offerings while celebrating and rewarding risk taking at the same time. In the past, when change was slower, you could prosper just by being efficient. Not any more.

You should also ensure that you do more than simply pay lip service to celebrating risks. This can be achieved by defining clearly what sorts of risks are acceptable, by whom and in what contexts as well as how you are going to reward them. Celebrating risk taking means making some public display of risk taking, giving equal glory to those who fail. There is no point just celebrating risks that turn into successes as this sends the message that it is O.K. to take risks so long as you don't fail.

3. Expose more managers to the outside world

Everyone knows the value of exposure to outsiders generally and to your market in particular. But what are the psychological reasons why too much internal focus undermines adaptability?

Part of the answer is that organisations are rather incestuous, leading to psychological inbreeding. This entails a vicious circle of stale ideas. Moreover, familiar routines go hand in hand with working alongside familiar people. Too much internal focus makes outsiders as foreign as new ideas. A further point is that managers who are too wrapped up in what is going on inside the organisation are too dependent for their career success on what happens internally. Managers who circulate widely outside the organisation can see more alternative career options for themselves so they can be more confidently independent. For them, therefore, risks taken internally are not as threatening as they might be for managers who depend too much on the organisation for their career survival. An analogy would be the dependency of state-owned organisations on the state and their associated resistance to change. Direct exposure to market forces leads such organisations to stand on their own two feet or go under. If they succeed, they will gain in confidence, just as the individual manager will become more independent through extra direct involvement in the outside world.

Managers who circulate widely outside the organisation can see more alternative career options for themselves so they can be more confidently independent.

Again, our virtuous inconsistencies rear their head in protest. Managers who must devote the majority of their effort to efficient delivery of today's offerings, will of necessity, be more internally occupied. The important thing here is for all concerned to recognise that these managers will need more active support in adapting to changes. Profit maximisers and cost reducers are essential to business success and should not be treated as bureaucratic dead wood by their innovation-loving colleagues.

Another way in which organisations are incestuous is through their reluctance to import any more managers from the outside than they can avoid. So many executives, even today, regard it as a profound failure if management talent has to be imported at senior levels rather than sought from 'home grown' sources. When managers regard internal positions as theirs by virtue of some 'right', they are too dependent on that organisation for their career success. This is a fail-proof recipe for impression management and defensiveness. Internal competition for positions is a better way to motivate managers to ensure that their services are up-to-date.

➲ **All of these forms of incestuousness have the same result: protect the status quo, keep it in the family and stick together even if it is not working.**

4. You get what you pay for

If you want people to make the effort to change, to be more adaptable generally, you have to reward them for it. We have already referred to rewarding employees for taking risks, but too many organisations see the implementation of change as merely a matter of exhortation and clear communication. What people are really held accountable for is how well they deliver immediate, bottom line results. This short-termism provides a ready excuse for managers to set aside longer-term change efforts. Each manager's annual performance appraisal, what he is fundamentally held accountable for, must give equal weight to major change efforts. Otherwise they will not happen. Changing entrenched habits and going against one's political grain takes too much effort to happen spontaneously when it is so easy to let other priorities push the long term into the background.

Outstanding examples of change efforts by teams and individual managers should be publicly rewarded to create role models for others to follow.

5. Pilot projects and phased change initiatives

Again, the idea that good communication is the key to paving the way for change, assumes that managers are rational or logical in some wholly mechanical, non-emotional fashion. All you have to do, it is assumed, is present them with the facts in favour of change logically and clearly. Being rational, they will adapt. Getting managers involved in planning changes is a well-known technique for enhancing commitment, but pilot projects are not so widely used.

The advantage of pilot projects is that they give people a chance to experience new processes before having to commit themselves to them. So, instead of selling the idea first – appealing to their brains – get them doing something new first. Often, they will find for themselves that the new way is better.

The psychology of this approach is that we make decisions about what we like to do on the basis of doing things that we then find we like rather than the other way round – deciding we like something first, then adopting it.

The same rationale applies to phased changes. The theory of personal transitions offered by William Bridges is based on viewing transitions as all-or-nothing events. But most changes do not need to be like this as we have seen. You can generally implement a new computer system, say, while keeping the other one going. This is the same idea as running a pilot project. In both cases, you are allowing managers to 'try before they buy.'

6. Foster a learning culture

Putting a premium on learning will not get beyond lip service either unless, again, people are regularly held accountable for learning new skills, new knowledge and new processes. Learning opportunities can also be provided, but, where possible, the more attractive ones should be used as rewards for desirable performance rather than simply freely available. As employees at all levels begin to cultivate a more entrepreneurial mindset, they will take more responsibility for their own learning. They will see their employers as their customers/market and, if they are to be successful entrepreneurs, they will be continually striving to keep up with your evolving needs. We are not there yet, however, in most organisations, so accountability will have to be used in the old-fashioned sense to foster ongoing learning – before supplier-customer accountability takes the place of the current boss-subordinate one.

A learning culture is impossible without regular feedback and coaching. As much as possible, managers should be encouraged to think like suppliers of services, as entrepreneurs. They will be more likely to seek feedback and coaching from internal customers when they begin to think like entrepreneurs. Objective feedback from a wide range of sources is hard to deny and regular feedback is the best antidote to defensiveness. We simply find it easier to accept feedback when we receive it regularly. It is really only the shock of unexpected feedback that causes people to be counter-productively defensive.

> *A learning culture is impossible without regular feedback and coaching.*

7. Eradicate excessive dependency

One of the major reasons managers resist change, as we have seen, is fear stemming from excessive dependency on the organisation to look after them. If you have no options, then you depend on things working out for you where you are and you cling to what you have got. Empowerment helps in this regard as it gives lower-level employees more confidence. The current emphasis of employee development on creating employability is another good step in that it provides people with the incentive to work with you in exchange for acquiring marketable skills. Career streams that include secondments with suppliers, customers and strategic partners would also be a positive action to take. While you may object that you are risking losing good people by these means, you cannot keep them by building a Berlin Wall around them either. Better to empower them so they feel as free to stay as to go. Tearing down the Berlin Wall did not empty East Berlin after all.

➲ Keep reminding yourself that dependency equals fear and fear equals clinging onto the status quo. The cost of excessive dependency in terms of increased resistance to change is surely greater than the cost of losing employees that have become too empowered to stay with you.

PRACTICAL STEPS

➡ New Year's resolutions to change bad habits won't get you very far beyond the New Year.

➡ Construct ways of getting recognition for your new habits and seeing that your old habits are punished.

➡ Highly-public commitment to change and regular monitoring will get you a lot further than any New Year's resolution.

➡ You are not really managing if all you do is fight fires – hence don't let short-term pressures sabotage your longer-term change goals.

➡ Hold a habit change competition with a colleague or friend who is also trying to change.

➡ Don't let the need for consistency across the organisation get in the way of real differences and complexity. All parts of the organisation do not need to adopt the same change goals.

➡ Celebrate risk taking – even those risks which fail – acknowledging all blind alleys you take in making decisions to destroy the defensiveness that is born of fear of failure.

➡ Develop an organisational culture that is more open to outsiders – more managers looking outwards and more outsiders being invited in.

➡ Develop the habit of trying changes before adopting them, letting your first-hand experience be the guide rather than relying exclusively on your exalted reasoning powers.

➡ Create a learning culture, one in which all employees think like entrepreneurs motivated to devote whatever time they need to in order to keep up-to-date.

➡ Help to make employees less dependent on you so they won't feel an obsessive need to cling to the status quo.

SUMMARY

Bad habits are maintained because they are comfortable and because the organisation rewards them in some way. Reasoning is not strong enough to kill off inertia. You need elaborate structures and processes, even if they seem a bit contrived. Essentially, you need to ensure that new behaviours are rewarded and bad habits punished. This means public monitoring and regular feedback. It is also critical to focus change efforts on where change is needed. Not all parts of an organisation need to change the same habits. While maintaining consistency where it is essential for efficiency, you should proactively work to avoid the rigidity of excessive routine elsewhere. This means shaking things up regularly through continuous exposure to anything or anyone different.

This chapter has dealt with some skills that could be useful in avoiding getting stuck with obsolete habits. In Chapter 6 we look at the sorts of skills that managers should cultivate to really excel at change.

'A generous and elevated mind is distinguished by nothing more certainly than an eminent degree of curiosity.'

Samuel Johnson, quoted in Boswell's *Life of Johnson*

THE SKILLS
OF A CHANGE
MASTER

OBJECTIVES

- To spell out some of the personal skills or competencies that managers should cultivate to excel at change.

- To provide suggestions on how managers can develop themselves in these areas.

INTRODUCTION

Having virtually exhausted the causes of resistance to change, we will now look at what it takes to change and adapt successfully. You are keen to be in the vanguard of all of tomorrow's changes and you have made plans to get rid of all your change-resisting bad habits. Now the question is: 'What positive skills or personal traits should you cultivate to ensure that you are as adaptable as you will need to be?'

Once we have identified a likely set of personal traits or skills and defined each of them fully, we will take a look at how you can develop yourself to be better at displaying each of them.

Finally, we will review the ideas we have discussed with regard to change in order to prepare for Part 2 of this book which deals with some of the harder specific changes managers have to face or will have to deal with in the future.

HOW A CHANGE MASTER MIGHT BEHAVE

Here we are not talking about change management regarding the ability to manage large-scale change projects. Our concern is with what it takes to be *personally* adaptable. Hence the term change *master* rather than change agent or change manager. Instead of talking of skills or personality traits, we will refer to 'competencies' – which are simply dispositions to behave in a certain way. A competency is a combination of skill, knowledge, personality and motivation. A good competency profile should be set out in behavioural terms, describing how a manager would behave rather than how he would feel or what his underlying personality might be like. It is also useful to break a competency profile down into positive and negative indicators, where positive indicators describe how a change master would behave while negative indicators describe how a change resister would behave.

The following competency profile is based on my experience working with, and assessing, a wide range of managers across several industries and organisational levels. It is not based on any hard research, so it must be seen as suggestive rather than in any way definitive.

The change master's competency profile

Each competency is first defined in terms of change receptiveness and adaptability. Definitions stay as close as possible to the ordinary meaning of these terms but may differ slightly. Following the list of defined competencies, the list is repeated with positive indicators (change master behaviours) and negative indicators (change resister behaviours) likely to be associated with each competency. There is no significance in the order of the competencies below.

1. **Resilient** – bounces back from setbacks positively and quickly.

2. **Opportunistic** – quick to recognise and capitalise on breaks.

3. **Accountable** – places self on the line and reacts non-defensively.

4. **Curious** – continuously seeks new information and learns new skills.

5. **Selfless** – consistently puts the interests of the organisation first.

6. **Self-critical** – regularly analyses own behaviour to improve effectiveness.

7. **Adventurous** – forsakes comfort zone to experience other perspectives.

8. **Communicating** – openly shares critical information with colleagues.

9. **Initiating** – instigates changes without waiting for direction or approval.

10. **Imagining** – thinks laterally and creatively, quick to see new angles.

11. **Innovating** – regularly generates and implements new ideas.

12. **Forward looking** – looks to the future without dwelling on the past.

13. **Visioning** – regularly displays awareness of longer-term objectives.

14. **Improvising** – spontaneously alters course to manage the unexpected.

15. **Networking** – circulates widely inside and outside the organisation.

16. **Market focused** – responds quickly to market/environmental changes.

It is unlikely that any one individual would display all of these behaviours and unrealistic to expect it. You or your organisation might want to pick a manageable subset to work on developing rather than trying to tackle the whole lot.

Positive and negative indicators for the above profile

1. Resilient – *bounces back from setbacks positively and quickly*

This competency deals with how managers *react* to setbacks as distinct from how they take 'initiative' or make themselves 'accountable' (see below), which are more proactive behaviours.

Positive indicators:

- consistently looks at the positive side after setbacks
- perseveres to find a way around seemingly insurmountable obstacles
- takes criticism positively
- picks self up and moves forwards quickly after losing battles.

Negative indicators:

- dwells on misfortune, sulks or withdraws to lick wounds after setbacks
- easily defeated, quick to muster excuses
- reacts angrily to the slightest criticism, seeks revenge, holds grudges
- over emphasises the negative impact of setbacks, sees only the downside.

2. Opportunistic – *quick to recognise and capitalise on breaks*

This competency is also *reactive*, like 'resilience', so it is less about proactively seeking or generating new possibilities as you would do if you were 'initiating' or 'innovating' (see below).

Positive indicators:

- often the first to pick up on opportunities for competitive advantage
- takes risks to capitalise on narrow windows to act
- regularly sees ways of pulling together non-obvious themes
- quickly spots, and takes advantage of, weaknesses in competitors.

Negative indicators:

- consistently advocates a 'wait and see' approach
- wants to be absolutely certain before taking even moderate risks
- visibly loses confidence and hesitates when faced with possible risk
- advocates letting competitors try new ideas first.

3. Accountable – *places self on the line and reacts non-defensively*

This competency has to do with having the necessary self-esteem or confidence to take risks and to accept failure gracefully without making excuses or seeking always to place blame elsewhere. This manager is keen to learn from mistakes. It complements the reactiveness of 'resilience' but is the more proactive willingness to put yourself on the line.

Positive indicators:

- publicly commits self to risky or potentially unpopular courses of action
- takes full ownership for own actions and their consequences
- willingly acknowledges own mistakes, highlighting what has been learned
- examines criticism constructively to see what further can be learned.

Negative indicators:

- consistently takes the safe course of action, keeps a low profile
- quick to place blame anywhere else but on own actions
- reacts to criticism defensively
- regularly complains about what 'they' have or have not done.

4. Curious – *continuously seeks new information and learns new skills*

This competency relates to the interest in continuous personal improvement and the desire to learn new skills. Such managers are always asking curious questions of all who will listen and spare the time.

Positive indicators:

- reads insatiably within a wide range of business periodicals and books
- consistently seeks to broaden self by inquiring into new developments
- seeks out and queries experts in a wide range of fields
- regularly takes on new projects to acquire new skills.

Negative indicators:

- spends all spare time exclusively on hobbies and other personal interests
- has little to contribute when others discuss upcoming developments
- shows reluctance to take courses or read anything business related
- employs primarily the same skill set/knowledge base year after year.

5. Selfless – *consistently puts the interests of the organisation first*

Being 'selfless' is not about being invisible or self-effacing, it has to do with putting others first, realising that one's success depends on serving others and enhancing their success, and especially that of the organisation as a whole. Such managers are not overly self-protective or inclined to wage turf wars.

Positive indicators:

- consistently acts in the interest of internal and external customers
- regularly sacrifices own goals to further those of the organisation
- continually seeks to refocus discussions around the organisation's welfare
- defuses conflict between others by reference to organisational goals.

Negative indicators:

- regularly wages turf wars, jealously guards own 'rights'
- demands that others conform to his agenda or needs
- gets angry at any request to compromise
- generally sees self as right, never wrong.

6. *Self-critical* – *regularly analyses own behaviours to improve effectiveness*

This competency complements being 'curious' except that here one's curiosity is directed inwards, so that you are continually examining your own behaviour to see how you can improve your own effectiveness.

Positive indicators:

- regularly seeks feedback from others on personal improvement efforts
- is well aware of own defensive tendencies and works to guard against them
- examines favoured processes publicly, inviting critical examination
- consistently observed to be trying to improve own effectiveness
- regularly asks searching questions about why he does things this way.

Negative indicators:

- accepts feedback only reluctantly, never actively seeks it
- regularly reacts defensively and shows no awareness of doing so
- tends to defend favoured practices, never scrutinises them critically

- never questions why he employs particular processes
- shows no evidence of striving to improve own effectiveness.

7. Adventurous – *forsakes comfort zone to experience other perspectives*

Being 'adventurous' is more proactive than just being 'opportunistic' – which is reactive. It is also more risky than merely being 'curious' as it entails taking on projects where you could easily fail for lack of direct experience.

Positive indicators:

- regularly takes on high-risk projects despite little direct experience
- quick to try new approaches and initiate off-the-wall ideas
- often the first to sample new technology or new developments
- celebrates diversity and fosters constructive conflict.

Negative indicators:

- clearly prefers familiar territory; role changes remain within a narrow band
- advocates the tried and true; cannot seem to see benefit of novel ideas
- adopts new technology or other developments only as a last resort
- wants a great deal of persuading or reassurance before trying anything new.

8. Communicating – *openly shares critical information with colleagues*

'Communicating' openly is related to being 'selfless' except that it specifically pertains to sharing information freely rather than monopolising it so you can develop a personal power base.

Positive indicators:

- freely answers every question about own activities and knowledge
- actively works to disseminate critical knowledge throughout the business
- takes steps to make it easier for others to gain access to key knowledge
- strives to ensure dialogue rather than one-way communication.

Negative indicators:

- tells others nothing beyond what he thinks they need to know
- hoards knowledge and actively prevents others from gaining access
- communicates only in a limited, one-way fashion
- regularly 'packages' information to make the impression he wants.

9. Initiating – *instigates changes without waiting for direction or approval*

Clearly you can't be 'accountable' or 'opportunistic' or 'curious' without taking 'initiative', but you can take 'initiative' in situations that do not precisely fall into these three categories, just to get something done, so it is a different set of dispositions.

Positive indicators:

- fixes problems without waiting to be told
- acts in accordance with organisational objectives independently
- solves major problems on own and makes major decisions comfortably
- instigates changes regularly to improve performance.

Negative indicators:

- sticks to job description unless specifically asked to do something novel
- excessively asks for approval or guidance when facing anything unfamiliar
- makes no changes other than those directed by others
- offers no suggestions on how to improve own or business performance.

10. Imagining – *thinks laterally and creatively, quick to see new angles*

This competency is about the ability to offer creative ideas, to think laterally. 'Innovating', by contrast, can involve quite practical actions. 'Imagining' has to do with seeing problems from unusual angles.

Positive indicators:

- regularly surprises others with ideas no one else thought of
- in problem-solving situations, often comes up with unusual angles
- regularly the first to pick up and understand novel ideas
- regularly poses creative 'what if?' scenarios, stimulating others.

Negative indicators:

- ideas and suggestions tend not to stray beyond the obvious
- regularly seems stumped when faced with difficult problems
- tends to find unfamiliar ideas hard to grasp, strange and a bit irritating
- quick to dismiss creative ideas as impractical, ridiculous or frivolous.

11. Innovating – *regularly generates and implements new ideas*

'Innovating' is not the same as 'imagining'. If you are 'innovative', you are quick to put new ideas to practical use. It requires you to be 'opportunistic' and 'accountable', but it relates specifically to turning good ideas into new products, services or processes.

Positive indicators:

- quick to turn vague ideas into practical process improvements or products
- often sees ways to make new uses of old practices, services or products
- usually one of the first to adopt new processes or techniques
- implements new ideas with unusual speed.

Negative indicators:

- has difficulty translating ideas into practical usage
- rarely goes beyond fine tuning of existing processes or products
- very slow and cautious about implementing new ideas
- strongly advocates retaining familiar, proven methods.

12. Forward looking – *looks to the future without dwelling on the past*

To be forward looking is to be optimistic, to see the upside in situations rather than dwelling on the past. It is to be always on the look out for a better way of doing things. Such managers may not be high on 'imagining' or very 'innovative' but they are quick to adopt the innovations of others. It is a bit like being 'resilient' except it does not have to do with your reaction to setbacks. You can also be 'forward looking' without necessarily being 'opportunistic' Similarly, you could be 'opportunistic' while being rather pessimistic much of the time.

Positive indicators:

- displays a positive attitude about own and organisation's ability to succeed
- continually encourages the search for better ways of doing things
- discusses ideas critically but works hard to tease out benefits
- focuses on what can be done better in discussing performance lapses.

Negative indicators:

- dwells on how good things used to be in the old days
- argues that this is the way we have always done it
- first to see why something won't work – dismissive
- seeks to blame and focus excessively on why mistakes were made.

13. Visioning – *regularly displays awareness of longer-term objectives*

'Visioning' is a bit like 'imagining' except that the latter is a bit undirected. 'Visioning' involves regularly painting long-range, big pictures about what a group or the entire organisation could become. It is not about having a vision in the sense of a fixed goal, but rather the inclination to constantly look for interconnections in the way the world is evolving.

Positive indicators:

- continually relates day-to-day issues to long-range plans
- displays enthusiasm for what a group can become in the future

- regularly presents big picture scenarios to explore alternative futures
- regularly draws others away from the detail to look at the broad picture.

Negative indicators:

- consistently immerses self in detail and the short term
- shows difficulty in discussing what lies beyond today's issues
- monitors and checks the work of others a bit obsessively
- never takes time to consider underlying reasons for immediate decisions.

14. *Improvising* – *spontaneously alters course to manage the unexpected*

To 'improvise' means to think on your feet, to be willing to cut corners or red tape as necessary to get the job done. It also implies the flexibility to switch priorities quickly and to respond creatively to the unexpected.

Positive indicators:

- cheerfully drops own plans and priorities when faced with urgent demands
- quickly abandons an approach as soon as it is clear it won't work
- redirects efforts as soon as new information comes to light
- thinks on feet, never stuck for an answer.

Negative indicators:

- is visibly upset when asked to change own plans for priorities of others
- difficult to approach without an appointment
- tends to be completely thrown by anything unexpected
- sticks excessively long with an approach despite its failure to work.

15. *Networking* – *circulates widely inside and outside the organisation*

'Networking' is quite different from the other competencies, so there is little concern about overlap. To network is simply to mingle and to pick up intelligence from all available sources – mostly relevant, some not so. 'Networking' is like 'communicating' only more wide-ranging.

Positive indicators:

- makes time to talk to a range of internal and external contacts
- demonstrates up-to-date knowledge about what a range of people are doing
- invites input from outsiders into his issues
- makes effort regularly to make useful new acquaintances.

Negative indicators:

- relates only to a small circle of colleagues and acquaintances
- tends to be one of the last to learn of new developments
- consults only the same people whenever he has an issue to discuss
- makes no effort to acquire new contacts.

16. Market focused – *responds quickly to market/environmental changes*

Being 'market focused' just means being externally focused and quick to change direction in accordance with changes in what the market and your competitors are doing. You could be 'opportunistic' and pick up mainly on internal opportunities, so these two competencies do mean something different. Also the 'market focused' manager may take damage limiting action which is not quite the same as seizing an opportunity. In other words, you could also be 'market focused' without being opportunistic.

Positive indicators:

- actions are clearly governed by a keen awareness of current market activity
- regularly draws the attention of others to what is happening in the market
- keeps up with what existing and potential competitors are doing
- focuses much of own activity on how to improve market advantages.

Negative indicators:

- preoccupies self with what is happening within the organisation
- cannot readily supply up-to-date knowledge of competitors
- shows little or no awareness of the latest market developments
- main interest is in generating personal political leverage.

DEVELOPING YOURSELF TO BE A CHANGE MASTER

Can you walk on water?

No one would expect you to be able to display all of the above competencies to the same exemplary degree. Keep in mind our earlier discussion that all organisations have two fundamental purposes or functions that are almost diametrically opposed:

- to deliver today's profits – this requires efficiency and sticking to procedures
- to renew, innovate, and create future products or services.

Just as these functions are opposed – another of our virtuous inconsistencies – so must those managers be different who work in them. Those in the delivery function need to be consistent, detail conscious, error avoidant, cautious and willing to work with routine. This function is mechanistic, however much you might find it personally interesting, in that it needs to be reliably the same over good durations of time.

Some managers will specialise in one function or the other. In reality, however, many if not most managers will need to shift between one hat and the other.

⮆ **The point to be noted here is that you need to determine for yourself which of the change competencies really apply to you in your role in order to decide which ones to major on in terms of your development. You should also take account of your current profile of strengths and weaknesses.**

So, for example, if your role requires you to be more 'opportunistic' than you could ever be, then there is little use in your beating yourself to death trying to be something you cannot be. In this case, it is better to ensure that you have someone on your team who can make up for this deficiency on your part.

In fact, this competency profile could be looked at as a team profile almost as easily as an individual one as long as no member of your team is so devoid of any of these competencies that he will drag the team down. That is, you can't quite take the view totally that it is O.K. if no single individual has all these competencies so long as the team as a whole has them. Clearly you won't be much further ahead if the change competencies are spread across four members of an eight-person team, given that you will need to get the whole team to change, not just half of it. Still, you might get by as long as every team member had strengths in a respectable number of competencies.

In what follows, ideas elaborated in earlier chapters will be further clarified by being organised under competency headings to make the suggestions for development part of a more coherent whole – a more total theory of personal transitions.

Development suggestions for each of the competencies

1. Resilient – *bounces back from setbacks positively and quickly*

The more you try to protect yourself from setbacks, the more severe will be your reaction to them when they do strike. Immunisation is the best developmental course of action in this case. Venturing forth, taking more risks and experiencing more setbacks is part of the answer. Another part is to work on changing how setbacks are regarded in your culture. Setbacks are in the eye of the beholder. If there is such a thing as an 'average' setback, it will be seen as nothing in a culture in which mistakes are celebrated and as a major personal disaster wherever mistakes are just not on. Further, regardless of your culture, you can work on cultivating a different attitude to setbacks by focusing simply on how things have changed for you when you 'suffer' a

> *Diversification means ensuring that you always have options, so you don't break all your eggs when you drop your only basket.*

setback – as neutrally as you can and looking for opportunities arising out of your changed circumstances. Clearly, some managers will find this easier to do than will others. Also, becoming more externally focused will help you to be less dependent on whatever happens to your career internally. Finally, diversification is another good strategy. This means ensuring that you always have options, so you don't break all your eggs when you drop your only basket.

2. Opportunistic – *quick to recognise and capitalise on breaks*

The first step to becoming more opportunistic is to get your nose into a lot of places where you can sniff out opportunities. You won't find them by daydreaming or navel gazing. This ties in with 'networking' and being 'curious' as discussed below. It means circulating and keeping in touch with what is happening in your internal 'market' and in your organisation's external market. The second step is to work at taking more risks. This does not entail being more risk-orientated in general, say by taking up gambling or throwing money at the stock market, but analysing your likely opportunities for career growth and taking risks merely in these areas. As the advice under 'resilient' suggests, however, make sure you have a range of options. The greater number of realistic options you have, the lower the risk of a serious setback if any risk goes bad on you. Again, immunisation should help in that the more times you stick your neck out without getting decapitated, the more comfortable you will be in seizing more risky opportunities.

3. Accountable – *places self on the line and reacts non-defensively*

As we have said before, the main reason you react defensively is that you feel vulnerable when attacked. If someone questions you out of complete ignorance of the benefits of your action, you feel on solid ground when you point out your reasons. You don't feel defensive in these situations. You respond not merely with confidence but with sadistic glee at making your attacker look stupid! So the key to making yourself less defensive and more accountable is to learn to feel on solid ground regardless of whether you might be wrong or not. This entails convincing yourself that making mistakes, for the most part, doesn't really matter – assuming your mistake is not so great as unintentionally launching World War III. You can always pat yourself on the back for having the guts to stand up and be counted, even if you are wrong sometimes.

4. *Curious* – *continuously seeks new information and learns new skills*

It is no doubt hard to cultivate curiosity if you don't really have it. A lot of managers are only interested in controlling a smoothly running operation well enough so it stays that way. They are not interested in new developments except in their favourite sport or TV sitcom. The pressure to keep up is so great now, however, that few managers can afford the luxury of any such complacency, unless you are in the sort of function or industry which changes little and the key to success is simply consistent maintenance of a required level of efficiency. If you can't make yourself more curious, the best you can do is allocate a set amount of time a week to finding out what's new. Without a set time, it won't happen. To keep up, you can choose the least painful means for you: talking to someone with more natural curiosity, asking a staff assistant to produce readable digests of the latest news, reading one trade publication, accessing a manageably sized internet site, or whatever other approach appeals to you.

5. *Selfless* – *consistently puts the interests of the organisation first*

Unlike curiosity, most people should be able to raise their selflessness a bit. It is simply a matter of continually striving to separate out your interests in seeing a particular initiative adopted from the interests of the organisation. While such striving may be easy enough to do, the ability to succeed in seeing the organisation's interests as varying from what you think they are is no mean feat. One step you can take is to canvass others, those who you know to be disinterested in the particular issue at stake. Here the key is to listen without arguing, striving to really understand how others could see things differently from you. There are times when selflessness is marginally less difficult to achieve – when you know you are fighting a turf war, for example, or undermining a colleague simply to get revenge. At least you should be able to see at these times that your behaviour is not in the best interest of the organisation. The advantage to you of always putting the organisation first is that you should then be less likely to react personally to setbacks, hence adapting more quickly. If, on the other hand, you take every setback personally, you will always be dragging your feet out of wounded pride and to get even. This style will make you resistant to change as you will be too emotionally hooked on the way things are or the way you personally think they should be.

6. Self-critical – regularly analyses own behaviours to improve effectiveness

This is one of the more important ones, partly because awareness of the need is a necessary first step to making any change. It is also hard to do on your own. None of us can see ourselves as objectively as we can see others and even that is not easy. Regular feedback from others is essential if you are to acquire anything like an objective perspective on yourself. There is no point, however, in asking your colleagues to give you feedback on the same old questions year after year. Ideally, you should be constantly striving to improve yourself in specific areas and requesting feedback from others on how they think you are progressing. There is no use, also, in shying away from asking potentially embarrassing questions.

> **Regular feedback from others is essential if you are to acquire anything like an objective perspective on yourself.**

7. Adventurous – forsakes comfort zone to experience other perspectives

Being 'adventurous' differs from being 'opportunistic' partly in being more proactive, but also in pertaining more to taking on challenging or stretching projects whereas seizing opportunities relates more to adopting new practices, processes, products or services. If you are 'adventurous' you will volunteer to get involved in unusual projects that lie outside the realm of your experience and which are not at all cut and dried. The parameters could even be quite ambiguous. You should have an easier time of becoming more 'adventurous' if you are working on being less risk averse generally. Again, immunisation applies. The more adventures you launch yourself into and survive, the easier it will become. The benefit to you is that your confidence and ability to cope with the unusual will naturally grow, making you more adaptable and receptive to unexpected changes.

8. Communicating – *openly shares critical information with colleagues*

Knowledge is power and the knowledgeable will be even more powerful in the future as our whole economy becomes more knowledge driven. Giving away knowledge is certainly to give away power. If you want to maintain a decent level of influence, you cannot give away all your knowledge unless you are constantly acquiring more. Here you are faced with a virtuous inconsistency on a personal level: you need to give knowledge away in the interest of team work and overall organisational effectiveness, but you need to retain some to keep a hold on your ability to influence. As with our organisational virtuous inconsistencies, it is a matter of getting the balance right. Customers are increasingly getting access to some company databases. For example, Fed Ex allows customers access to their logistics system to track down their own parcels.

Savvy companies are seeing benefits, from a customer service point of view, if they give more data away. To strike the right balance, you can pass on information and retain influence by subtly ensuring that you get something in return, if only an I.O.U. If you are striving to be selfless as well, your guide will be the question of what is in the organisation's best interest. The idea is to convince yourself that you will win in the long run if your customer (your organisation) wins. What has this got to do with making you more adaptable, you ask? It is not so much that communicating more fully makes you more receptive to change in and of itself. It is rather that doing the opposite, hoarding information, is symptomatic of the sort of selfishness that will make you resistant to change.

9. Initiating – *instigates changes without waiting for direction or approval*

Initiating is simply a matter of seeing yourself as a supplier of services, as an entrepreneur, so that you are constantly thinking of what other, or new, services you can offer your internal customers. It also has a customer service element: the desire to astonish your internal customers by giving them more than they expect. To become more initiating, you should strive to look for ways in which you can add extra value instead of just sticking to your job description. Treat your boss as your most important customer and work at keeping in touch with his issues, looking for ways you can help out. This is a particular way of being 'selfless' and will enhance your adaptability because you will train yourself to think more of your customer's needs than you do of your own. Hence, when demands to change come your way, you will immediately see this as an opportunity to offer new services to your customer rather than wallowing in self-pity because your world will no longer be the same.

10. Imagining – *thinks laterally and creatively, quick to see new angles*

This is a very hard one to develop. Some of us, if not most, simply cannot think this way. Your best bet may be to ensure that you have an off-the-wall thinker on your team whose lateral thinking ability you can plug into. Maybe some of it will rub off on you. There are books and courses on lateral thinking, but these will at most make you more receptive to crazy ideas. You should strive to achieve at least this level of 'imagining', however. Keeping it in perspective, it is also important to note that not all functions will need this degree of creativity. Also, as we noted earlier, it would be self-defeating to undermine your confidence generally by beating yourself to become something you cannot be. Courses and books on creative thinking should also help you to stop and think when faced with problems to see if you cannot come up with a wholly new perspective. Even if you do not succeed often on your own, it will be clearly worth the effort occasionally. Moreover, trying to think creatively as a team may be easier for most of us than trying to do so completely on our own.

11. Innovating – *regularly generates and implements new ideas*

To be innovative, you do not really need to come up with original ideas yourself. You just need to be quick to apply them as others have done or to see new ways of applying them to your processes or products. Of course, the more innovative will also devise their own new products, processes and services. A first step is to keep abreast of new developments and to develop the attitude that you want to be one of the first to implement new ideas. If you are ahead of the game, you will generally be more adaptable whereas if you are always the last to pick up on new developments, your attitude will always be 'Here we go again!' One of the reasons managers are resistant to change is simply because they resent being last, seeing colleagues getting ahead of them and adopting ideas they feel they should have thought of themselves. So, when they resist such changes, they are really expressing frustration with themselves for having already missed the boat. This is hard to admit, of course, because we need to dump our bad feelings onto some other source external to ourselves.

12. Forward looking – *looks to the future without dwelling on the past*

To be more 'forward looking' is difficult if you are the pessimistic type as you will tend to expect the worst of your future. Pessimism is a global attitude in the sense that the pessimist sees everything the same way. Even if you cannot rid yourself of your global pessimism, you may be able to develop more optimism in some respects. The key is to break everything important down into two categories:

● those things that you feel you must be pessimistic about, and
● those things you feel a glimmer of optimism towards.

To do this, ask yourself, of each scenario, what is the best possible outcome. Strive to elaborate as many benefits as you can. Being pessimistic is just a disposition to see the downside of every situation more fully and more immediately than you see the upside. While you may not divest yourself totally of your pessimism, you may be able, through effort, to see more upsides than you would naturally tend to see. Being 'forward looking' is also about constantly looking to improve things, to have the attitude that you can always do better. If you are 'forward looking' it will be easier to be 'self-critical', because you will be motivated to improve yourself by the feeling that you could indeed be better in some respects. If you are pessimistic, on the other hand, you may always feel that you were better off in the past. This attitude clearly is not conducive to adaptability. However hard it may be to be more 'forward looking', the first step is to convince yourself that you do have a choice with regard to how you view things.

13. Visioning – *regularly displays awareness of longer-term objectives*

This is a bit like being 'forward looking' except that is involves the contemplation of concrete alternative futures. It is not about having a crystal ball to see the future, nor is it the setting of rigid, unchangeable long-range targets. It is really a matter of striving always to relate what you are doing today to some pertinent bigger picture, however frequently that may change from year to year or even from month to month. We tend to think that a vision has to be unchanging. But if it is so unchanging these days it may be so abstract as to be unrelated to anything you are doing in the here and now. The underlying attitude of someone who is 'visioning' is that we are going somewhere and it is worthwhile toiling to get there. To be more 'visioning' is merely a matter of taking the time regularly to ask yourself how what you are doing supports what the organisation is trying to achieve. This outlook should make you more receptive to change as you will then be more constantly in tune with the bigger picture and hence less wedded to your own narrow patch and less taken aback when new processes come your way.

The personal development action here is simply to set regular time aside to think about, and discuss with others, where you are going as a group.

14. Improvising – *spontaneously alters course to manage the unexpected*

To be 'improvising' is another way of being 'selfless' because it involves being responsive to the needs of others and their unexpected demands. The less 'selfless' person is more concerned with his own needs – his desire to stick to his plan and his timetable. Again, it is a matter of getting the balance right, of being organised but not so caught up in only your own agenda that you become inflexible. Here the personal development action is simply to work at redressing the balance slightly so that you do not see red when someone asks you to shift your priorities unexpectedly. Catch yourself saying, 'Do you mind if I just finish this first?', and practice just dropping what you are doing to help someone else out, convincing yourself in the process that it is not the end of the world if you have to come back to your priorities a bit later. Cultivating an internal customer-first attitude may help you to set aside your own agenda without feeling so imposed upon.

> *Cultivating an internal customer-first attitude may help you to set aside your own agenda without feeling so imposed upon.*

15. *Networking* – *circulates widely inside and outside the organisation*

As with a few of the other change competencies discussed already, this one is relatively easy to develop, being mainly a matter of setting aside the time, recognising that nothing short of time formally set aside will do. Strategically, as time is at a premium, you should identify people within and outside the organisation from whom you have most to learn. Clearly, you need to be able to offer useful intelligence in return. A good idea would be to agree to have lunch periodically with specific people for the express purpose of helping each other keep up-to-date with some important aspect of your internal and external markets.

16. *Market focused* – *responds quickly to market/environmental changes*

Last, but certainly not least, being 'market focused' is about staying close to your market, even if this is an internal one. If you are in the finance function, let's say, your market is all the internal customers you serve. Staying close to them involves keeping abreast of their evolving needs for financial information rather than hiding away in your ivory tower and guessing what refinements might be a good idea. To be more 'market focused', you could do well by being better at 'networking', but it is more than this. It is cultivating the attitude that the services you offer must always be tailored to the needs of your market otherwise you could find yourself out of business one day. Like 'networking' it is a matter of setting aside time to maintain close contact with your key customers and trying to anticipate their needs. Again, by putting your mind in this frame, you are less likely to be caught off guard by major changes in your market.

SO WHO IS A CHANGE MASTER?

Possibly no one will be a change master if it means being a wizard in all of these competencies. The essential thing is to achieve relative proficiency in as many of them as you can while ensuring that your team can cover the rest. Help each other out on the weaker areas that each team member can do nothing to correct.

PRACTICAL STEPS

➡ Expose yourself to new ideas and people so you won't be hit by them.

➡ Take more risks to immunise yourself against the fear of failure.

➡ Diversify by learning new skills so you will be less wedded to anything.

➡ Change the way you view setbacks – work to see new opportunities.

➡ It's easier to stick your neck out with a less tragic view of mistakes.

➡ Set aside regular time to soak up new developments in your field.

➡ Be less wrapped up in your own needs – think: organisation first.

➡ Regularly get tough feedback for an honest review of how good you are.

➡ Volunteer for off-the-wall projects to stretch your imagination.

➡ Avoid hoarding information – don't take yourself quite so seriously.

➡ Keep close to internal customers to find new ways of adding value.

➡ Strive to think more laterally or get close to someone who finds it easy.

➡ Work at being the first to apply innovations and to devise your own.

➡ Avoid dwelling on the good old days, look to create a better future.

➡ Take regular time out to fit what you are doing into a broader picture.

➡ Be organised but also willing to improvise, to shift direction fast.

➡ Make time to network with at least a few strategically chosen contacts.

➡ Know who your key customers are and keep abreast of your market.

SUMMARY

This chapter has listed a number of personal skills or competencies that managers should cultivate to excel at change and it has provided some suggestions on how managers can develop themselves in these areas. While this list is based on experience rather than anything approaching scientific research, you can be sure that many of the competencies are close to the mark. Without question, cultivating a thoroughgoing entrepreneurial attitude will make you better able to cope with change in the future and, indeed, become a change leader.

In Chapter 7 we begin to look at how to be more effective in dealing with specific transitions, starting with one of the most poorly managed: getting promoted to a senior position in a different organisation.

WHERE ARE WE NOW?

Thus far we have reviewed a good number of the reasons why managers fear or resent change. We have looked at what to do about inertia on both a personal and organisational level as well as how to change deeply ingrained habits. Now we have rounded the picture off by detailing the sorts of behaviours you should cultivate if you are to be as adaptable in the future as you would like to be.

Without doubt, the real crux of everything we have covered up to this point is the need for every manager to begin thinking more like an entrepreneur albeit one who happens to work in a big organisation. This means thinking less like an employee in the old-fashioned dependent sense of that term. Thinking like an employee – at the deepest level – is basically thinking like a child in the sense that you depend on your organisational parents to protect you and to not let you down. Much of resistance to change is not a million miles away from rebelling against parental authority.

So, if you want to keep one image in mind to help you to remember the various suggestions made here, then think of yourself as an entrepreneur and all that such an image implies with regard to keeping up with the future, if not ahead of it.

➲ **You will not regard change as a trauma if you are better prepared for it and if you cultivate an entrepreneur's attitude towards it.**

WHAT NEXT?

As role changes are among the hardest changes for managers to accept gracefully, we now need to apply what we have covered thus far to see how some specific personal transitions can be negotiated more successfully.

'A man of great common sense and good taste, meaning thereby a man without originality or moral courage.'

George Bernard Shaw, *Notes to Caesar and Cleopatra*

PART 2

CONFRONTING THE HARD TRANSITIONS

'On him does death lie heavily who, but too well known to all, dies to himself unknown.'

Seneca, *Thyestes chorus*

REACHING
FOR THE STARS

OBJECTIVES

- To understand why the 'new broom' sweeps out inherited subordinates and brings in a new team.

- To see how this move amounts to a failure to cope with change on the part of all concerned.

- To devise ways of managing major personal transitions more effectively.

INTRODUCTION

This chapter is a practical chapter and using the example of Frank Thompson, the 'new broom ', allows us to study the dynamics of a particular set of changes. What we learn from this study can help us negotiate all personal changes more successfully.

THE FAILURE OF THE NEW BROOM

 Frank Thompson felt a mixture of elation and just a bit of anxiety as he accepted the offer to become Operations Director in a bigger company, a major food processer. In his more elated moments, he felt as though he could conquer the world. In this frame of mind, he could hardly wait to take over his new position, to establish his authority and to make his mark.

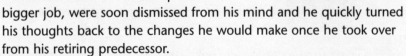

His slightly anxious moments, when he wondered whether he was up to the bigger job, were soon dismissed from his mind and he quickly turned his thoughts back to the changes he would make once he took over from his retiring predecessor.

At times, he could scarcely believe his luck at winning the competition for such a prestigious position over three external and two internal candidates. He had been with his current employer for 20 years and, at age 45, was beginning to wonder if he had reached the highest rung of his career ladder. But as his company was the market leader, he was seen as the brightest prospect for a company that was a distant third in the market. The knowledge that he was coming from a company with superior manufacturing processes gave Frank confidence that he could show his new colleagues a thing or two.

His new boss, the Chief Executive of the firm he was moving to, had to do a thorough selling job on his prospective colleagues to justify hiring him as it was very unusual to bring in an outsider at this level. Much to Frank's astonishment, he was greeted with a mixture of barely disguised hostility from some of his new colleagues and a wait-

165

and-see attitude from others. Frank was a bit hurt, as well as shocked, at the coolness of his reception in light of the Chief Executive's treatment of him as a sort of saviour.

Frank's initial reaction shaded into a tinge of self-doubt as he wondered whether maybe he was the wrong man for the job. Thanks to the Chief Executive's support, however, Frank's self-doubt and hurt soon turned to anger. While his management style had been very participative in his old company, he was not at all uncomfortable calling the shots when the chips were down. On the rare occasions when he needed to, Frank could tackle difficult people and other obstacles quite aggressively.

The Chief Executive had hired him to turn things around quickly and Frank soon had a clear handle on the major problems besetting his new operation. Seeing so clearly what needed to be done, combined with his anger at his cool reception, motivated Frank to attack issues with a more no-nonsense aggressiveness than he would normally use.

At the same time, Frank felt acutely the pressure and high visibility of his new role. It felt as if the whole company was watching him and discussing his every move. Frank knew he had little time to do something before losing credibility. The Chief Executive had so played up Frank's talents that many of his new colleagues felt quite a lot of scepticism about what he could accomplish. The anxiety to prove himself fast only fuelled his resolve to take aggressive action in order to make his mark and establish his authority quickly.

Frank used a particularly belligerent tone with his Manufacturing Manager, John Clark, who was one of the defeated internal candidates. He also took a hard line with Owen James, the Quality Manager, who had not been a candidate for Frank's job. Both of these managers had been with the company for over 20 years and they were both a few years older than Frank. John Clark was naturally disgruntled at not receiving the promotion that his former boss had led him to believe he would be getting. In Owen's case, he felt such loyalty to his former boss that he had difficulty warming to Frank immediately. While he tried to be helpful by pointing out certain 'facts' to Frank, it became increasingly clear that Frank was seeing him as an awkward character.

After a few frustrating months, Frank began to realise how much he had relied on his old colleagues in his previous company to co-operate with no questions asked. Now he was met with open resistance or at least many more questions than he was accustomed to having to answer. This made Frank feel quite lonely at times and to start thinking about bringing in his closest allies from his previous company to help him here.

After six months of battling on alone, Frank fired John Clark and Owen James, citing their resistance to change as justification. This was a stunning shock to his new colleagues who were unused to firings at this level and who had seen John and Owen as change agents previously. How, they wondered, could change agents be seen as resistant to change? As soon as he got rid of his 'enemies', Frank poached new Manufacturing and Quality Managers from his previous employer. Several more departures, voluntary and otherwise, took place before things settled down and Frank's operation started to see improvements.

In the meantime, the company had lost further market share due to the mediocre quality and high cost of production of some of its major products. An independent management consultant cast doubt on whether the company would ever recover its lost ground despite Frank's belated, if substantial, achievements.

A familiar tale?

All too familiar, you say? Who hasn't observed this scenario at first hand or been on the receiving end by now? With the exception of large-scale downsizings, many enforced departures at senior levels are the direct result of someone's getting a new boss from outside the organisation within the past 18 to 24 months.

Almost without exception, acquired subordinates are seen as legitimate scapegoats. If the organisation needs turning around, someone must not be up to the mark and deserves to be pushed out, or so it is felt. Moreover, what could be more damning than being judged resistant to change? Note that it is always the acquired subordinates who are so condemned. The incoming saviour is never so regarded: he is seen as the supreme architect and exemplar of change. The sweeping out of an existing management team, all or in part, is so common that we have jargon to label it with: the 'new broom' is what we call any senior executive who joins an organisation from elsewhere.

What is really going on here? Why is the 'new broom' himself never seen to be shabby at coping with change?

FLOPPING IN A BIG PROMOTION

The theme of this chapter is that newcomers at senior levels, as well as their acquired subordinates, are equally hopeless at managing such a major role change. Both are to blame for the ensuing bloodshed because neither has a clue about the underlying psychological forces pulling at their puppet strings and determining, all too predictably, how they will react.

➲ **The essential point here is that all managers will increasingly have to manage major role changes in their careers and the move to a bigger job in a new organisation is one of the hardest. By analysing why this role change is handled so poorly, perhaps we can figure out how all role changes can be more effectively negotiated.**

You may be objecting that, in your view, Frank handled his transition perfectly well. What else could he have done under the circumstances, you wonder? Frank's transition was a failure not in view of his taking a bit longer than expected to turn the situation around, but because he failed to integrate effectively into his new role in the first place. And his new colleagues, especially his new subordinates, failed equally miserably to adjust to his arrival. Hence, Frank failed doubly as he had no idea how to help his new colleagues adjust to him.

So, what went wrong with Frank Thompson's transition to the big time? Let's first list the pressures he was under, the potential causes of anxiety that could have undermined his ability to reason clearly:

- no previous experience with transitions of comparable magnitude
- the Chief Executive's exaggerated sales pitch to justify bringing in an outsider created impossible expectations and formidable scepticism
- the sheer visibility of the role was naturally anxiety-producing due to its importance and just the fact of being a newcomer
- any elevation in status is to lonelier territory and inevitably creates some anxiety about possibly failing in all but the super-confident

- winning a desirable position over a tough competitive field will nearly always generate some scepticism among all but avid supporters
- the need to prove yourself quickly can lead to anxiety driven, hence hasty, decisions, making you look foolish and creating more anxiety
- further, the need to prove yourself quickly can lead you to impose your 'superior' knowledge on others actually *creating* resistance
- loss of one's previous support group makes such an elevation in status doubly lonely, leading to more anxiety
- combining a slightly anxious state with such loneliness makes the slightest coolness on the part of new colleagues seem like rejection
- even neutral or indifferent subordinates can thus be seen as enemies
- getting rid of perceived 'enemies' is an emotional, defensive reaction which, however, buys time and provides you with any excuses you may need for not delivering all that is expected.

One of the most important messages in this catalogue of disaster generators is that Frank's anxiety-led, aggressive approach actually contributed strongly to creating the resistance to change among his subordinates that he then used as the prime reason for getting rid of them!

Failing to adjust to a new boss

Before looking at what Frank could have done differently, let's look at what went wrong with the reception given to him by his new subordinates:

- they reacted childishly, like children rejecting a suddenly imposed step-parent – loyalty to the lost parent cannot be quickly set aside
- the Chief Executive's hard sell created expectations that few, if any, managers could live up to, fuelling more reticence than there might have been otherwise with softer, more realistic positioning

169

- a new boss imposed on people feels like a setback to those who had a good relationship with the predecessor – now you have to start over

- any subordinates who aspired to the position will be most disgruntled

- even those who try to be helpful by pointing out why something 'isn't the way we do things around here' can be seen as being too critical, difficult or unfriendly

- even children will reject a newcomer if he tries to assert any authority over the group too quickly, that is, before being fully accepted

- high expectations are bound to be disappointed when the newcomer acts precipitously showing how little he understands the new culture

- a disappointed expectation transforms initial coolness into hostility.

However much this transition failure can be blamed on newcomers and inherited subordinates, the Chief Executive, other colleagues and the human resources function all played their part. Hence, all could play a role in easing such transitions. Let's look first at what Frank Thompson could have done differently.

GETTING PROMOTED WITHOUT FALLING ON YOUR FACE

 What could Frank have done differently?

Frank should have approached his new job by taking account of the emotional upheavals he was bound to face. He may have needed some coaching on this as he hadn't experienced any transitions quite so massive as yet in his career. Nevertheless, he had been promoted numerous times before and he might have extrapolated from this experience more thoughtfully instead of simply basking in the glory of his victory and contemplating the wonder of his forthcoming rule.

He might then have negotiated a more sensible set of expectations and a more reasonable period of time before he would have to deliver. Upon his arrival, he could have positioned himself as being, at least partially, in a learning mode simply to open himself to listen to others rather than being so quick to ram home his 'superior' knowledge. He could also have taken more of a leadership stance, positioning himself as determined to get the best out of his new team rather than simply implementing his own ideas.

He could have held extensive team-building sessions with his new subordinates, going out of his way to help them mourn the loss of their respected former boss and to adjust to a newcomer. He might have flattered them a bit if he had understood that they were feeling somewhat rejected and undervalued due to their own lack of advancement. The team-building effort might have created a cohesive team – vital before any major initiatives could really get off the ground.

While Frank undoubtedly did have invaluable experience, thanks to working in a more successful company, he could have endeavoured to generate ideas for improvement out of his subordinates, *leading* them to draw his conclusions rather than imposing or selling his ideas to them. His behaviour would then have been that of a genuine leader rather than simply that of a functional expert. The problem for Frank here is that, under pressure, we tend to regress to an earlier stage of our development. So, although Frank had developed good leadership skills in his previous job, he forgot them because of his anxiety and reverted to his old comfort zone, that of an engineering expert. In his older comfort zone, Frank felt less anxiety and was hence comfortable forcing through changes that his new team was resisting.

Without wasting time, Frank could have exerted more effort to build a new support network among his peers. Instead, Frank was hurt by their cool, wait-and-see attitude, so he withdrew from them with an I'll-show-you mentality. This made him determined to go it alone to prove what he could do without their help, surely a disastrous move.

If Frank had been in better touch with the effects of his own anxiety on his ability to think clearly and to make sound decisions, he might have taken steps to relax a bit rather than proceeding so precipitously. A slightly more relaxed, if still urgent, approach might have led him to consult a bit more widely before initiating so many changes so quickly, some of which had to be aborted at the cost of some of his credibility.

Frank also wanted to prove to his former colleagues at his old company that he was going to make a great success of his new role, so he cut himself off a bit too much from them. He felt that discussing problems with his closest former colleagues and mentors would be an admission of failure so he chose to tough it out alone until he could poach some of them to replace his rejected subordinates. If he had maintained just a bit more of an open dialogue with his closest ex-colleagues or mentors they might have helped him to keep things in better perspective.

 ## Support from your boss

What could Frank's boss have done differently?

The Chief Executive's major mistake was in over-selling Frank into the new position. Like Frank, his own handling of the situation was more anxiety-driven than rational as well. He knew he had to take drastic action to protect his own job and he recognised that an outsider would not be accepted readily. No time could be wasted, he felt, in easing Frank into the position, so he opted for a hard-sell approach in the hope of completely dissolving any opposition to the idea of an outsider coming in at this level. The result was actually to increase scepticism and to put Frank under even more pressure by making him so much more visible. Instead, he should have checked his own anxiety and saw the need for a reasonable integration period for Frank.

Further, he could have positioned Frank as just bringing an outside perspective, not a superior one. To achieve this more constructive positioning, he could have created the impression that he thought internal candidates were indeed world-class managers, but still argued that even a world-class management team can become stale in today's fast-changing world without the injection of the occasional breath of fresh air. Instead, the Chief Executive went out of his way to maintain that no insider was up to the job, hence creating more resentment and resistance than there would have been otherwise.

The Chief Executive could also have demonstrated more leadership by holding team-building sessions with Frank and his new peers to foster stronger relationship building rather than leaving it totally to Frank to feel his own way with his new colleagues.

Because the Chief Executive created such unrealistic expectations for Frank to fulfil, he made it next to impossible for Frank to talk to him openly. How could Frank speak to him about any difficulties he was having when the Chief Executive had made him seem infallible? Team building sessions in an off-site location might have enabled Frank to open up more readily with his new boss as well as some of his new peers. Such relationships would have undoubtedly reduced some of the pressure on Frank and provided him with at least one reassuring confidant and source of support.

Support from your new team

 What could Frank's inherited subordinates have done differently?

Frank's ablest subordinates rightly saw themselves as candidates for the job he got. No doubt this is a hard one to swallow. But as we have seen in earlier chapters, to react to such a setback like a hurt child is totally self-defeating however hard it may be to respond in a more constructive, adult, entrepreneurial fashion. If they had been fully versed in the way that irrational emotions can block receptiveness to unwelcome changes, they might have bent over backwards to welcome Frank and to help him settle into his new role quickly. They might have seized the opportunity to serve a fresh customer and positioned themselves as being on his side instead of against him – or at best indifferent to his success.

His new subordinates might have realised that, no matter what good ideas Frank could bring to the company, he would still need them, that only team work could achieve anything. They might have also appreciated his anxiety to prove himself and helped to reassure him instead of watching for mistakes.

If his subordinates had seen Frank as a customer, they might have openly asked him what his needs were and how they could support him, rather than passively waiting for him to act. But they didn't see themselves as entrepreneurs, they saw themselves as dependent employees in the old-fashioned sense, hence totally at the mercy and whim of their organisational superiors. Operating within the traditional parent-child mindset that still permeates most organisations, they reacted like children instead of like adults.

A little help from your friends

 What could Frank's peers have done differently?

Frank's peers should have acted more like entrepreneurs as well instead of like tribal chieftains wondering how they would be able to compete successfully with this interloper for top level attention. They might then have seen Frank as a team mate and sought him out to offer their services. This would have been entrepreneurial of them as they might have formed some useful alliances with Frank. This approach would have given them a competitive advantage in their battle within the internal market. Instead, their behaviour towards him was anything ranging from cool to mildly hostile.

HOW CAN THE CULTURE HELP?

In a more supportive culture it would have been a more common practice to import outsiders into senior positions in the first place. They would have cultivated a less macho, win–lose atmosphere where too much emphasis is placed on individual excellence. In such a culture there would be a healthier balance between team work and individual effort.

➲ **A culture that could fully welcome an outsider would be one which cultivated more external exposure and influence all along, with more managers taking secondments elsewhere and more movement in and out of the organization generally.**

If your only option is up or out (or sit and fume), then too much is at stake in such a culture – hence the destructive level of competition.

Any help from human resources?

Perhaps the human resources (HR) professionals are most to blame for their failure of leadership. They saw their part in Frank's success as ending once the recruitment process was over. Induction and integration of employees is something they would think of applying only to junior staff. True leadership on their part would have amounted to fostering a smooth integration for Frank. They would have coached all key stakeholders on how to adjust to what is surely a major change in their circumstances. Their coaching would have applied to all concerned parties, including Frank and the Chief Executive, as well as Frank's subordinates and peers. A request for support from colleagues would not have been positioned as a need to help Frank – that would have undermined his credibility. Rather, their support would have been explained as a need to rebuild the team surrounding Frank's function as quickly as possible. Such a leadership intervention on the part of the HR professionals would have made everyone concerned see the issue as a change management problem, not as anything to do with any weakness on Frank's part.

But no one did any of these things, so there was a massive leadership vacuum, one that no one made any effort to fill. Hence the usual cycle of deteriorating relationships ensued, followed by the usual, costly and acrimonious blood letting. Despite the hard lessons, no one was any the wiser after this experience and Frank went on to repeat the same mistakes the next time he moved on to a bigger job elsewhere.

Of course, none of this is to say that dumping inherited subordinates is never justified, but its near inevitability surely means that many such situations are down to anxiety-related failures to cope with major role changes.

WHAT ABOUT OTHER ROLE CHANGES?

How can we extrapolate from Frank's failure to other role changes so that we can learn how to handle any shift in responsibilities more effectively? Not many role changes are as significant as Frank's in terms of magnitude and pressure. But analysing Frank's role change is like putting all role changes under a microscope: it enables us to metaphorically blow up the emotional dynamics involved because, in Frank's situation, they are so obvious. Less major role changes will engage some of the same emotions, but they may be too slight to be so easily observed. Despite their lower visibility, however, their effects could be just as damaging.

What we need to do now is examine the major factors contributing to Frank's errors to see how they might apply to all significant role changes.

First of all, clearly the sheer magnitude of a role change is always going to be one of the major factors that will test your adaptability. But how do you decide whether a role change is huge or small given that magnitude will be very much in the eyes of the beholder? What might be a shattering role change for me could be a piece of cake for you. Also, the difference between the two roles cannot be experienced in abstract terms, you can only experience the change in context.

➲ This means that two role changes of equal magnitude will be experienced differently depending on how supportive you find the context to be, not to mention other pressures that will surely vary enormously from one role shift to another.

So, what was it about Frank's role change that made it a major one for him? He had certainly experienced other big promotions within his old employer without seeing them as traumatic. A critical factor making Frank's role change so significant was the extra visibility he had to manage. Getting promoted and moving to a key role in a new company creates much more visibility than just getting promoted in your own company. In the latter case, your rise is not usually so surprising. If people expect you to move up, they are hardly so likely to be watching intently to see if you fail. Frank's sudden rise in visibility was more than this, of course, it was also the pressure to deliver quickly so as to avoid losing credibility.

➲ Clearly then, it is the combination of high visibility and high expectations that can create so much pressure and place so much stress on your change-coping abilities.

Another critical factor is the reception you get in the new role. Suppose you are elected nearly unanimously to be President of your social or sports club. Being elected so emphatically, you are surrounded by avid supporters. In Frank's case, it was like getting elected by one sports club to run the opposition's club!

➲ Who's going to welcome, as their leader, someone from the enemy camp?

These considerations show that the magnitude of your role change is really a function of all of the factors that could contribute to making your adjustment difficult. It is not simply a matter of how different are the responsibilities between the two roles.

Coping with everyday role changes

Let's see how these points might apply to a more mundane role change.

EXAMPLE

Suppose you are the Marketing Director in a medium-size division of a large conglomerate and you are promoted to the position of General Manager over the division as a whole. This is an easier move than Frank 's but not as cosy as your nearly unanimous election at your sports club. Here you will have more opposition to confront: all those in other functions who think that one of their own should have been promoted.

But people cope quite well enough with such changes as these every day, you object. When the pace of change is slow, yes this may be true enough, but in the future when younger people are promoted even faster than they are today to ever-more stretching responsibilities, promotions that are so easy may be few and far between.

Nevertheless, it will be illuminating to see how we can take what we learned from Frank's failure and apply it to a promotion that is so commonplace that most managers, apparently, handle it well enough. The Marketing Director's boss still has to do something of a PR job to convince the rest of the division to accept someone from a different function. Let's assume that his predecessor had an engineering background. After taking over the new position, the now 'ex' Marketing Director will not feel quite so alone and the resistance he experiences from his new subordinates will not feel quite so threatening. The problem here, however, is that there is still resistance from some of his inherited subordinates, only it is too hidden to really confront. In this case, the new General Manager is less likely to feel a need to fire anybody, but the resistance he experiences is nonetheless real and strong enough to be very costly.

Over the first two years, the new General Manager may find it hard to introduce major changes in the operations side of the division because the manager in charge of this function cannot see what a marketing know-it-all can know about manufacturing. As time goes by, the pressure to improve the performance of the division may rise to the point where a much more aggressive stance is taken, again at greater cost than might have been necessary had the new General Manager integrated effectively. Part of the problem here is that the resistance is too subtle to be noticed initially, so the situation is perhaps even more expensive long term than Frank's. Because resistance is not noticed, two years of efforts to change can be lost before it is realised that change initiatives are being deliberately put on a back burner.

Consider an even smaller role change.

Suppose you are moved from the Information Technology department of one division to the same department of a sister division. It is felt that you would benefit from learning how a different division uses information and they, in turn, would gain from your specialised knowledge. Even here, the same emotional forces that undermined Frank could sabotage your seemingly routine change of roles.

Let's say your arrival in the sister division is positioned by your new boss as a need to 'straighten out some problems', so an 'expert' from another division needs to come in. As your mandate is to clean up a mess fast, you begin to make definitive suggestions immediately. How do you suppose this well-intentioned help will be received? Not likely any better than Frank was appreciated. But who has failed to cope with change in this case? Surely all concerned, just as in Frank's case. Your new team mates were hooked emotionally by being made to feel that an outsider had to come in and sort them out. Your new boss set up an emotional trap for you to fall into. And you fell into it by being 'helpful' before getting yourself accepted on their terms first.

THE NEED TO PLACE BLAME

A really intriguing question arising out of all this discussion is:

➲ **Why don't managers see these issues as being about coping with change?**

178

Frank didn't see his difficulties as having anything to do with his ability to deal with change. Neither did the Marketing Director, nor our IT professional. For all of them, the problems were simply caused by the pigheadedness of the particular people they had to work with, either as subordinates or team mates.

Why is this? Psychologists have long since discovered an interesting fact about how we attribute the causes of our feelings. If you do something laudable, you see it as down to your intelligence and other superior personal qualities. If, on the other hand, you do something stupid, you attribute the cause of your blunder, not to yourself, but to circumstances outside of you: somebody or something made you do it. What's really interesting about this face-saving strategy is that we reverse the attributions completely when we explain the behaviour of other people. Here, if someone else does something praiseworthy, we are often tempted to see their action as due to circumstances rather than their intelligence: they were in the right place at the right time, it was an accident, or some other factor prompted them to do it. Conversely, if they do something stupid, we nearly always see their action as due to their own inherent stupidity, almost never because of circumstances outside them.

So, Frank and the other role changers, blamed their difficulties on the people who most closely confronted them, seeing them as pigheaded rather than under the influence of heavy emotional strains and circumstances. In Frank's and the Marketing Director's cases it was inherited subordinates whose stupid resistance was due to their inherent stupidity and, in the IT professional's case, the problem was stubborn peers. To add fuel to the fire, if there are real performance problems anyway, it is easy to see this as extra evidence to support your initial diagnosis of inherent stupidity.

> If you do something laudable, you see it as down to your intelligence and other superior personal qualities.

The other problem here is that, when we are emotionally engaged, i.e. angry and frustrated, we react immediately to any emotional provocation. While we may be good at analysing technical problems in considerable depth in order to identify underlying causes, we simply throw our analytical abilities out the window when it comes to understanding the reasons for emotional confrontations from other people. If people attack us, it is clearly, we feel, a matter of some deficiency of character on their part. We hardly ever stop to think whether forces in the context have provoked them to be so irrational.

As a result, we react just as emotionally in return. This is because we see the individual as *personally* attacking us. We don't see a whole set of surrounding circumstances attacking us, it's just this terrible person who is against us. And because we react just as emotionally, the detached reasoning skills we use to analyse technical problems in great depth completely desert us.

Moving beyond blame

The truth of the matter is that our behaviour, as well as that of everyone else, is always determined partly by our own predispositions and, in addition, the circumstances in our environment. Knowing that we are strongly biased in the direction of over-crediting ourselves for our praiseworthy actions, we can perhaps more objectively acknowledge that we are often driven more by circumstances and the actions of others than we normally care to admit. And we must, in fairness, extend the same understanding to the blunders of others.

➲ **For our purposes, the bottom line here is that to cope with change we need to manage a whole host of contributing environmental factors as well as our own emotional reactions to the sorts of provocations that so easily set us off.**

We need to be better at setting aside our own feelings and more rationally try to understand the underlying reasons why others behave as irrationally as they do sometimes. The logical understanding that a master of change should be capable of displaying would enable him to help others move beyond their own emotional triggers instead of being no more than a puppet on a string to them.

It is easy enough for us to see how circumstances in our immediate environment trigger our own emotional reactions, so it is simply a matter of extending this understanding to others. Once we fully make this move, we should be able to manage personal transitions more effectively.

 ➡ **As a first step, it becomes a matter of understanding the typical emotional reactions we and others are likely to display under what circumstances.**

➡ **Secondly, we than have to work at:**
- **controlling our own reactions**
- **arranging the circumstances so as to minimise our own emotional reactions and those of others**
- **helping others we encounter avoid also getting hooked emotionally.**

MANAGING THE CIRCUMSTANCES

Let's look at how you can manage the circumstances surrounding a role change to increase your chances of a successful transition.

1. Positioning your entry

Make sure that you are not positioned in any superior fashion to the people you will be joining in your new role, if indeed, you are actually moving to a new location or otherwise gaining wholly new colleagues. Ensure that you are positioned as someone who will complement an already strong team; someone who brings a different, not necessarily better, perspective; someone who has as much to learn from, as to contribute to, the existing team.

2. Managing your exit

If you have been with your current team for a good while, you will miss its support if you cut yourself off from it too completely. We often leave situations with negative feelings of one sort or another. If you couldn't wait to get out of an unpleasant job, leaving may feel like getting out of prison. In this state of mind, you may be in no hurry to remember your former inmates. Or, if you were quite happy in your job, you may feel guilty for abandoning your friends. Again, you may feel more like washing your hands of the situation than maintaining contact. But a complete cutting of ties increases the suddenness and finality of your transition, putting unnecessary pressure on you and increasing your anxiety levels. Such total abandonment of your former role increases your loneliness in the new role. Feeling this way is highly conducive to poor handling of any emotional roadblocks thrown in your path by others.

3. Managing your emotions

Here the key to coping with significant transitions is first to be aware of the likely emotional pitfalls you could fall into. You must expect a little reserve from others in the new environment initially, but be prepared not to take that personally. If you are an outsider, you will need time to be accepted. This means not imposing yourself on others, but seeing them as customers who you should bend over backwards to help. Seeing yourself as providing a service to them should put you in the right frame of mind. Your job, in the early days, is to sell your services and this means selling yourself by being as helpful and patient with them as possible. Where you perceive a more hostile reception, again, the key is to hold back from reacting emotionally yourself. The best course of action is to find a cool moment to have a quiet heart-to-heart talk with the disgruntled colleague. Chances are he has nothing against you personally, even if he mistakenly blames you for his feelings towards the change that you stand for in his mind. If you really succeed in controlling your own emotions you may be able to provide him with the patient and understanding coaching he needs to see that he is personalising matters that you really did not bring about.

4. Managing your entry

This step has already been touched on under managing your emotions. The key is to get accepted first before trying to impress new colleagues with your knowledge. Too many newcomers fail by trying to sell themselves through their expertise. They see the need to be accepted clearly enough. It is just that they don't realise the need to show some respect for the knowledge and experience of their new team mates first. The psychology seems to be somewhat related to territorial feelings. Those who have been there before your arrival see themselves as above you in some sense. They have been around the place longer than you and, whatever technical expertise or experience they may lack relative to you, they have knowledge of how their own team functions, its history and how 'things are done around here'. They, therefore, see you as a junior member of the team in this sense even if you are joining as their boss. Before you can assert either your formal authority or the authority of your superior knowledge, it is critical that you get yourself accepted on their terms. This means living through some sort of initiation period. When you see that their reserve towards you has evaporated and they can laugh and joke as easily with you as they can with each other, then you can assume you are well along the road to being accepted.

You would also be wise to ease into offering your greater wisdom. You can do this by gentle questioning of existing practices, asking whether trying this or that would be helpful rather than directly criticising any of their existing practices. Its also advisable to avoid citing the way you did things where you came from as well. The resistance you could cause by this line may take the form of suggesting you go back to where you came from if it was so great there. Whenever you sense that your advice is sounding like you think you know it all, you should ensure that you make some strong noises about how many useful ideas you are learning from their way of doing things. Playing down how great it was where you came from will make your new colleagues feel that their team is seen as an attractive place to be rather than as some prehistoric backwater. It is all about going out of your way to enhance or maintain the self-esteem of your new colleagues. They, after all, are competing with you to some extent for favours from their superiors and you can be seen as a potential threat even if you are joining them as a junior peer. Flattering them a bit reduces the sense of threat that they may feel. If you can put them at ease and still get them to adopt some of your ideas through sensitive and judicious questions, you are not only adapting well to change, you are demonstrating substantial leadership ability too.

> *Playing down how great it was where you came from will make your new colleagues feel that their team is seen as an attractive place to be rather than as some prehistoric backwater.*

PRACTICAL STEPS

This chapter has been very practical throughout. We have seen that role changes are hard to manage because they dramatically involve leaving something behind and starting over elsewhere. They are also hard because people need time to adjust to outsiders. Therefore:

➡ the 'new broom' transition has been swept under the carpet for too long: it needs to be seen as a failure to cope with change on the part of all concerned

➡ apply the hard lessons of the new broom transition, to all role transitions

➡ understand the emotional dynamics of all parties involved in order to manage role changes successfully

➡ the final step is to minimise the emotional pollution by managing how you leave your old role, how you are positioned to your new team and how you integrate into the new role.

SUMMARY

Your success in getting promoted will always be resented but that does not mean that you should take it personally. It will happen to everyone, no matter who they are. The key to coping with it is to depersonalise it and to see it as a function of circumstances, of how your entry is managed by you and other stakeholders. Your role as a change agent here is to help others, and yourself, manage the critical change. The promotion to a more senior position in another organisation is only the most visible and most poorly handled of major personal transitions. Studying the dynamics of such changes carefully can help us negotiate all personal changes more successfully. Even a lateral move is slightly resented, simply because you do not yet belong. Again, the reaction to your arrival would be the same no matter who you are. So, look at the circumstances instead of taking it personally.

Chapter 8 deals with another major personal transition that all managers are currently having to face – that is learning to live with less power as customers, partners and employees all gain a share of the manager's power.

'Next to enjoying ourselves, the next greatest pleasure consists in preventing others from enjoying themselves, or, more generally, in the acquisition of power.'

Bertrand Russell, *Sceptical Essays*

MOVING AHEAD
WITH LESS
POWER

OBJECTIVES

- To gain an understanding of how the power of managers is shifting to customers, employees and other stakeholders.

- To devise ways of coping with this potential mother of all personal transitions.

INTRODUCTION

The good news is that the only changes that are hard to cope with are the ones that force us to alter intense emotional propensities. The bad news is that fervently-held emotions are never easily shrugged off.

There are few, if any, more zealous emotional needs than the desire to hold onto waning power. Hence the common view that power is like a drug that clings to its addicts with an unshakeable grip once it takes hold.

Most managers, men especially, are motivated by the desire to gain power. Many will deny this, but then they are interpreting power in a narrow sense: the right to boss people around. In today's more democratic companies, a lot of senior executives will never admit to needing to boss anyone around, and maybe they really don't enjoy this aspect of their power. But the ability to command action through more subtle means is part of the satisfaction of having power. A high-status position in any hierarchy provides the holder with power regardless of how it is used. If nothing else, this is the power to command respect, to have a right to be listened to by your lessers, to have access to other sources of power, to be able to wield influence in all sorts of little ways. Perhaps, more than anything else it's the satisfaction of knowing that you have distinguished yourself from others, that you have arrived and made yourself the envy of your one-time peers.

In this chapter, we take a look at a major change that is still a bit on the horizon although many managers are starting to feel its effects. This is the shift, well under way now, of power from positional authority to the authority of knowledge and expertise. It is also about the growing power of other stakeholders, from customers to strategic partners. Many managers have already adjusted to the new found power of customers. Hanging onto the attitude that you can tell customers where to go rather than serving their every whim is as fatal today as having a deadly disease. But not many managers are ready yet to give away the same degree of power to subordinates. So-called empowerment should really be seen as the thin end of the wedge leading to a greater eventual shift of power to 'knowledge workers'. Without some understanding of this profound change, too many managers will go kicking and screaming before they relinquish their hold on the power they have spent a lifetime acquiring.

The cost of this resistance could be enormous, very possibly bringing down whole companies in its wake.

WHO HAS POWER AND WHAT IS IT?

In organisations, having power is unfortunately confused with holding down a position in a hierarchy. But an independent writer, lawyer, critic or management guru can have power just as well by virtue of his ability to command the attention of desired audiences. The benefits of having such power are the same as those accruing to positions in an organisational hierarchy: people will not only listen to you willingly, they will pay to listen.

Even the proverbial starving artist in his freezing garret wants power. He may think that he just wants to produce good art, but his definition of good art is partly dependent on how others receive it. Getting no recognition during his lifetime will hardly qualify as success for him no matter how much he esteems his own work. Power for the artist is simply the ability to attract the adulation of his peers and other art lovers. This is the power to demand premium prices for your work, to achieve financial independence and to avoid doing hack work. Most importantly, it is the power to make your mark and to be recognised as having achieved something not only remarkable but of lasting value. This is not the power of positional authority over others, but the ability to command respect from those whose esteem you value and it can be just as satisfying and every bit as compelling as positional power.

Great sports figures and film stars also have their own form of power. Their greatness is achieved through a combination of talent and hard work, just like anyone else's. The source of their power is again different from that of the senior business executive, but the personal benefits are no less tangible and no less valued.

The old saying about the corrupting influence of power is sometimes used to explain why those with high political office abuse their power for the sake of personal gain, but the real corruption is more psychological than criminal.

Power corrupts because the desire to avoid losing it seems to become so much stronger than the desire to acquire it in the first place. Once people have power, it often goes so much to their heads that they become megalomaniacs, striving to retain power by grabbing even more. At this stage, megalomaniacs think they have a *right* to the power that they competed with others to obtain in humbler times. The megalomaniac defends himself against fears of mortality by exaggerating, in his own head, just how powerful he is. This exaggeration is of course a defensive move to deny his own fading grip on things. In this overblown frame of mind, the megalomaniac treats people as if they were despicable insects. It is primarily by downgrading the status of others, psychologically, that the megalomaniac elevates, in his own mind, his own fading power.

What is power anyway?

In narrow organisational or political terms, power is usually considered to be *the ability to get people to do things*. This is too simplistic and is due to the unfortunate association of power with positional authority. But power comes in all sorts of other forms as we have seen. Yes, power may be the ability to influence people to do things for you, but not only via the right of positional authority. There is the sheer personal power of a charismatic person or of someone who is seen as highly attractive sexually. These people have power over others simply by virtue of their ability to attract them, to command the attention of others and to be able to get their wishes fulfilled simply by asking people to do them favours. Ultimately, this kind of power is the most compelling because it does not need the support, or the threat, of some form of potentially punitive force.

Power and resistance to change

The more you value anything you have gained, the harder it is to let go of it. Managers who have become used to having a lot of

191

Perhaps the desire for power is, at the most fundamental level, the desire to be attractive to potential mates.

power are most likely to resist any change that threatens to undermine them. The mighty do not see their power as a possession like an expensive car that is disposable, they see it rather as an inherent aspect of their personality, hence the feeling that no one has the right to take it away from them. For many top executives, their identity as the person who has all this power may be the most important feature of how they view themselves. So, it becomes not a question of giving up a disposable possession but rather of trying to become someone less attractive than you are now. And who intentionally wants to be less attractive than they are at the moment?

The connection made here between power and attraction is no accident. Many psychologists and evolutionary biologists believe that evolutionary success is based on reproductive success. So, perhaps the desire for power is, at the most fundamental level, the desire to be attractive to potential mates.

In any case, the more wedded you are to power, the more likely you are to have difficulty adapting to any change that threatens to take it away from you. This means that we can expect managers hooked on power to resist losing it in all sorts of creative ways, perhaps seemingly giving up some power here only to grab a bit more there.

Turning now to the concrete application of power in today's organisations, we need to look at the various ways in which power has already been seeping through the fingers of managers and then, how it is likely to further erode in the face of other, imminent changes.

Power already long lost

Let's begin with a look at how the power of managers at all levels in organisations has already been dissipating. Up to the last decade or so, successful businesses were like famous writers who could write anything they liked and whose readers bought anything they churned out. Such writers could afford to be disdainful of their public so long as their every scribble was in such demand.

Most businesses had the same arrogant attitude towards customers in all aspects of what, and how, they served customers, from product choice, design and quality, through delivery times, price and customer service. All stemmed from a we-know-what's-good-for-you stance. Similar attitudes towards employees also prevailed until very recently. As all production was labour-intensive, employees were treated as mindless robots who had to be monitored closely, perhaps patted on the back occasionally to stop them form complaining too much, but certainly not consulted on how to do business.

The more successful businesses could also relax as far as competition was concerned, because there was comparatively very little to worry about. Naturally, with no threat to their power, such organisations could behave just as they pleased. More than any other single factor it was growing competition that forced managers to change their tune; this combined with lightening fast communication technologies. Faster feedback simply speeded up the process of finding out what your competitors were doing in your markets, forcing you to shrink all your lead times. Sheer speed alone turned the drivers into the driven. Rather than constructing unshakable five-year plans like some monolithic communist state, large organisations were forced into a highly-reactive mode, anathema to the controlling urges of the once powerful.

The other impact of competition was, of course, to give consumers undreamed of choice. What better form of power than to have choice? How many people can simply choose to buy an expensive yacht and spend three months cruising around some far away Pacific islands? Not many have this choice nor, hence, this power. Nonetheless, the lowliest of consumers are spoiled for choice at any shopping counter they elect to visit, thanks to rabid competition for their attention. Now the consumer is just like a sports hero or film star: all these businesses are clamouring for their autograph on a cheque or credit card slip. So who has the real power here, the manager of the major business or the lowly consumer?

➦ **Regardless of how you slice it, a great deal of power the manager once had has irrevocably shifted to customers.**

Ironically, however, managers may not feel they have lost any power worth losing. They may have lost the power to foist any old rubbish onto customers, but more successful business leaders have learned that, if you discover the secret of what customers really want, you can gain back lost power in a new form. This is the power of being able to reap millions from giving people what they want. So perhaps there is a happy balance of power here rather than it being too one-sided for either the manager or the customer.

Losing power to other stakeholders

Governments regulate businesses far more closely than ever before, through all sorts of standards applied to product safety and quality, through laws against anti-competitive behaviour, environmental regulations, employee welfare and anti-discriminatory legislation. The list is endless and the end is not in sight.

Many businesses have now formed all manner of strategic partnerships with suppliers, customers, competitors and other related industries. Partnership entails joint decision making, hence less power in the hands of any one organisation or any one executive. Even once docile shareholders are now flexing their muscles more threateningly, causing once arrogant executives to cower for fear of losing their jobs.

KNOWLEDGE AND POWER

The rising power of knowledge workers

We have been bombarded over the past four or five years with talk of 'knowledge workers', employees with highly-developed skills and good education. Like the liberated consumers of today, knowledge workers seem to be demanding rights they never had before. Older Personnel Managers refer with undisguised revulsion to the way their newly-hired, university-educated employees demand to do certain types of work where once they simply did what they were told.

It is easy to see how business competition has given consumers more power, but what is the source of the apparently fast-growing power of the so-called knowledge worker? Well, they simply have more choice too. This is because industry as a whole is shifting from the mindlessness of manual labour to knowledge work, involving the transformation of complex data into other, equally intricate, forms. People who work with their heads are qualified to do so because of exotic skills and knowledge that are not as widespread in the general population as manual skills. This shorter supply of knowledge workers creates higher demand.

➲ **If you are in demand, like today's consumers, you automatically have more choice.**

But it is not just having a choice of where to work that has so empowered today's well-educated, it is rather the more important fact that so many more businesses are totally dependent on knowledge for competitive advantage. Here there are sharp industrial differences. If you are running a chain of laundries or fast-food outlets, where you can rely on lower-paid manual workers, you can still call most of the shots. Your power is not just the power over hiring and firing at will, it is the more critical power to determine how the business will be run at all levels.

The shift in power to knowledge workers will be most profound in those industries that are highly knowledge-driven: high-technology companies and fast-moving consumer goods industries, especially consumer electronics and computer-related products. There is a continuum of knowledge intensity from such industries to those that depend more fully on manual labour. In knowledge-intensive industries, detailed direction can only emerge from the heads of innovative product specialists – hence, less power for managers in these industries.

Maintaining today's business versus creating tomorrow's

There is another distinction of relevance here that somewhat parallels the one between manual and knowledge work: the difference between delivering today's products efficiently, on the one hand, and, on the other hand, creating tomorrow's products through innovation. We alluded to this dichotomy earlier, but it is

195

of prime significance here, because knowledge and innovation tend to go hand in hand. Industries that depend on manual labour tend to compete on cost, service and quality. They need mechanistic and mindless consistency in order to survive. Knowledge–intensive companies, such as those that create software products, for example, compete not so much on cost but on their ability to keep coming up with leading-edge, exciting products.

In organisations driven by cost pressures, senior executives have as much power over employees as they ever had in terms of fully deciding strategic direction on their own, regardless of how much power they may have lost to consumers and other stakeholders. By contrast, in businesses dependent on innovation, it is really down to the creative talents of your front-line technical people to determine the direction and success of your business. You may decide broadly that you want to major on internet software rather than PC software, for example, but the particular products you ultimately offer will simply have to emerge out of the minds of your knowledge workers. You have little or no real control over the shape of the particular products that will evolve.

In the old days, senior executives had much more control over their organisations' offerings. While they have lost the power to dictate what products they will sell, they still have the same sort of power of any customer. As internal customers, they can decide to buy one new product proposal over another, but even here, they will need the advice of those more closely in touch with the market than they can afford to be.

➲ **Those most up-to-date with market developments will be highly-qualified knowledge workers who must spend most of their time looking at how the market is evolving if they are to have any hope of leapfrogging the competition with new products everyone will want to buy.**

Implications of the shift in power to knowledge workers

Business is becoming much more democratic, thanks to the diffusion of power away from senior managers to all the other stakeholders we have mentioned. (Service businesses not so dependent on knowledge workers may actually become more autocratic under competitive pressure.) Customers, shareholders, government, joint venture allies and employees, all have become *partners* in your business as power has flooded in their direction over the past decade or so. What power do you now have as a senior manager if you are only one among several partners – all with different agendas?

As we saw in noting how managers have lost *dictatorial* power over customers but gained the power to be successful through giving consumers what they want, it is evident that the most resourceful managers will devise other sources of power. For instance, they now have the power of...

- the broker, facilitator or catalyst
- the customer
- the venture capitalist
- the sales person
- the leader
- the artist.

Let's look at each of these types of power in turn.

Managers as brokers

While managers can no longer dictate to knowledge workers, they can serve as a go-between to bring disparate groups of technical specialists together for specific projects, much like a film talent scout assembles a cast of appropriate stars to make a film. The role of the manager is now to facilitate communication between technicians who are often too specialised to communicate effectively with each other. As knowledge develops further into ever-increasing complexities, knowledge workers will need to specialise even more. Although empowerment may lead them to manage more of their work and think more entrepreneurially instead of relying so heavily on the organisation, there will still be a role for managers. Resourceful managers will bring teams of specialists together, acting as catalysts and facilitators instead of dictators.

> *Resourceful managers will bring teams of specialists together, acting as catalysts and facilitators instead of dictators.*

➲ **Managers will have to be more entrepreneurial to survive and this means sniffing out possible products and bringing the right specialists together to develop them.**

This is a networking and liaison job far more than a management one in the old sense of planning, monitoring and controlling. Actual project management will be done more by automated computer processes combined with more self-management. This part of the manager's role will largely disappear from his job description.

Managers as customers

Increasingly, knowledge workers will see themselves, albeit perhaps in a virtual sense, as self-employed suppliers of services, as entrepreneurs who have to sell their services continually to their employers in order to get onto the best projects. In future, the best knowledge workers, like film stars, may have agents hustling behind the scenes on their behalf – another possible role for displaced managers perhaps?

➲ **In the role of virtually self-employed suppliers of services, knowledge workers must learn to see managers as their customers rather than as their bosses. The manager as customer may then come to feel as powerful as today's consumers.**

Although this is a different form of power, it may still be just as satisfying. You may have to treat your stars with kid gloves just as film directors have to pacify the prima donnas of the film world, but you still have the power to buy one person's services over those of someone else.

Managers as venture capitalists

Venture capitalists are just customers with more money to spend. Having more money means having more power, of course, and it may be the image that most appeals to managers accustomed to enjoying substantial power. The suggestion here is not that managers will leave their employers and join venture captialist firms, but that their current roles will evolve away from hands-on doing towards the direction of investing in what knowledge workers propose to them.

➡ As a venture capitalist, the manager's role becomes one of adjudicating between major pitches for funds. The competing proposals will need to be well thought out and made as attractive as possible.

Regardless of the power of knowledge possessed by the competing presenters, they will all need to cultivate the goodwill of the venture capitalist. The more creative ones will be the best entrepreneurs. While executives turned venture capitalist will have the ultimate power to decide among competing proposals, they will depend on the proposers to shape the details of what they have to offer. Just as customers are limited to deciding whether to buy A or B, not to how A or B are constructed, so the manager turned venture capitalist will have a more limited form of power than executives of 20 years ago.

Managers as sales people

The more entrepreneurial managers will not so completely abandon their technical expertise as the stereotypical General Manager was supposed to do 20 years ago. They will stay close enough to their markets to look for opportunities. While they may not retain the level of detailed technical knowledge necessary to fully assess the feasibility of their new product hunches, they will have enough knowledge to sell their ideas to prospective teams of more technical knowledge workers. To use the film analogy again, the film producer or director often has to sell scripts to prospective stars in order to convince them to undertake a certain role. Managers with good sales skills will prosper in this role.

➡ The important point to note here, however, is the shift from *telling* to *selling*.

Managers will not be able to simply order teams of knowledge workers to get on with producing a fancied possible product. They may try, but be sabotaged in one way or another by powerful knowledge workers who will have more choices than they once had.

Managers as leaders

There has always been a lot of talk about how the best leaders excel by motivating people to think for themselves. For the most part, this idea has not amounted to much more than talk, simply because so many managers want to make the key decisions and tell people what to do. They don't like the more hands-off role of being a mere source of inspiration to others. But as the detailed content of major decisions falls more and more into the laps of knowledge workers, the true leaders of tomorrow will have no choice but to focus on inspiring unusual effort and synergy across diverse prima donnas. This role will combine some of the others we have just discussed, especially that of broker and sales person. Such leaders will recognise fully how little they know about what ought to be done to solve content problems and determine content direction, so they will be happier to deal with process issues: how to combine diverse inputs into the best possible united force.

➲ **Leadership in this context also entails negotiating with all the other stakeholders to create an environment in which knowledge workers have the best chance to excel. This sort of leadership depends exclusively on personal persuasiveness and not at all on the authority of hierarchical position. That is the fundamental difference between today's leaders and those of tomorrow's 'intelligent' organisations.**

Managers as artists

Consider again the comparison of the role of manager with that of the film producer or director. Once upon a time, we thought of management as a science, not unlike the science of engineering, for example. Some managers have always seen their work as an art form of sorts, but this has not been the dominant view. The art of the film producer is to turn a vision into a work of art by bringing together all the right elements and by creating an atmosphere that stimulates the creativity of the best talents. Because of the complexity of commercial products today, however, the executive may have only a dim vision of what the end product might look like. Nevertheless, such an executive is no less an artist because he will have to rely solely on personal skills to mould together so many divergent stakeholders into a creatively functioning whole. Just as the artist gains a type of power via the satisfaction of creating a product everyone admires and wants, the executive can take a similar pride.

➲ **Such executives will be in demand for their services as a result of their major successes and this is a different sort of power to the usual positional authority.**

200

COPING WITH WANING POWER

The pressure to retain control

The key to adjusting to any new role is to ease into it gradually. By easing into it you can find substitute sources of satisfaction before fully releasing your hold on your outdated comfort zone. Any all-or-nothing plunge into something completely new is going to feel awfully traumatic, inclining some managers to back away from the precipice and cling on to obsolete roles.

Letting go of power is doubly difficult today because of the enormous pressure senior executives are under. As we have seen earlier, pressure tends to cause us to revert to what we know best. Hence, the newly-promoted sales person is anxious about making the grade as a manager, so he devotes too much attention to what he knows he can do successfully and that is to keep selling.

Senior executives are less secure in their positions today than they have been at any time in the past. Competition, pressure from powerful stakeholders and immediate feedback on results, thanks to modern communications technology, means there is no place to hide for the harassed executive. In these circumstances, the executive's natural tendency is to exert more control, not less. It is only by staying close to the detail that the executive can feel on top of things, in some control over his fate. Generally, such a more hands-on intervention means getting involved in decisions that should have been delegated. This in turn calls upon the executive's knowledge of *content* as opposed to majoring on the use of facilitative skills and processes.

> *Senior executives are less secure in their positions today than they have been at any time in the past.*

Unfortunately, the executive is likely to be well out of touch with what to do in content terms. His need to have some control may then combine with his anxiety over having insufficient knowledge to make matters worse, hence leading him to take even more control – clearly a vicious circle.

How to gain power by giving it away

The essential step to making the transition from direct control to a less immediate form of power is to trust more fully in your own ability to influence others using only your personal persuasiveness. As a football coach, you cannot get onto the field and play the game for your players. You must sit on the sidelines and sweat it out, doing your best to guide, inspire and motivate. Senior executives who cannot quite bring themselves to retreat fully to the coaching role think they can save the day by donning their player's uniform again, even if only for one last charge. Surely this is a recipe for disaster and it will become even more so as business becomes increasingly knowledge-intensive.

➲ **The key point here is, therefore, to learn to sit on the bench and like it.**

The first step is to realise that the desire to return to the playing field is completely anxiety-driven, it is not at all a rational decision. Even if you do have some valuable playing moves to make, your presence on the field will simply distract your players and cause them to focus on you, thereby taking their eyes off the ball. So, unless you can do it all, better stay on the bench.

If you can resolve to scale down your anxiety, the next question is: What can you do to ensure that you feel busy, useful and able to exert some power in the situation? Broadly speaking, your role is to win over any doubters who are putting undue pressure on you among your various stakeholders and then to focus on delivering what you promised. Here, you need to restrict your role to coaching, drawing a sharp distinction between *doing* and *guiding*. Doing is making decisions that should be delegated. As soon as you start making these decisions yourself, you are effectively disempowering your subordinates, making them too dependent on you and undermining their confidence.

This means biting your tongue and forcing yourself to stay in facilitative mode. Just as a business can gain power by giving it away to customers, you can gain a new form of power by fully empowering your staff. By this means you are more likely to succeed, hence to please your customers (stakeholders) and hence to be asked for a repeat performance or, if you like, repeat business.

⊃ **Empowering people, therefore, means giving power away, but in giving it away you gain more (indirect) power.**

This sounds paradoxical, but is the result of essentially not using power in the short term in order to gain more in the long term. When your behaviour is completely anxiety-driven, you feel compelled to exercise power directly *now*, to start telling everyone what to do, to don your player's uniform once more. Everything becomes urgent because you feel out of control. Managing this emotional pressure can free you to display more patience, to give power away in the short term as an investment to gain greater power in return a bit down the road.

Being happy with less power

A major role change, as we have seen, is never easy. Some of the critical competencies you will need to call upon to move to a role with less power are among those we identified in Chapter 6: being 'resilient', 'opportunistic', 'selfless', 'self-critical' and 'adventurous'. Many of the competencies we discussed earlier are also those required by the successful entrepreneur. Being 'selfless' in this context means thinking less about your own loss of power and more about how you can benefit the organisation, your main customer. If you are 'opportunistic' enough, you will devise your own ways of adding value.

Start by being sufficiently 'self-critical' to identify what you can offer and to convince yourself to stick with the coach's role. And if you can become more 'adventurous', you may find yourself enjoying a new role. Like the entrepreneur, your environment is more competitive now in the sense that you cannot simply shrug off failures so readily as in the past when your position was more unassailable.

The benefit of living in a competitive environment, however, instead of dominating a monopoly, is that your victories are more satisfying. As with the football analogy, you should find beating tough competitors more satisfying than beating pushovers. Similarly, if you have to rely solely on your ability to influence a diverse group of powerful stakeholders to achieve success, then victory will be indeed worth celebrating. By way of contrast, surely

203

only the insecure could find it satisfying to get what they want simply by shouting at a herd of yes-men,

We said earlier that defensive face-saving could be very counter-productive, but we also likened it, in milder forms, to a healthy immune system. This is an essential part of the process of coping with a significant role change. In this case, it is a matter of convincing yourself to give up the power associated with being the strongest player on the field in exchange for the power of the coach.

➲ **The face-saving move here is to convince yourself that you are better off because it is actually a sweeter victory to influence those whose power is equal to, or greater than, yours than it is to dominate the powerless.**

Some defensive moves are not so productive. Executives who cannot cope with such a potentially devastating role change will be able to kid themselves only for a short while. They will achieve short-term success in knowledge industries perhaps by re-engineering processes and cutting costs. Their need to retain control will incline them to take short-term, immediate actions – anything that gives their fragile egos a sense of achieving something. They may even drag out their hold on old-fashioned power by moving on to greener pastures once they have taken all the short-term measures they can take in a knowledge-intensive business. They will be seen as a success in the eyes of many of their powerful stakeholders who also want, above all else, short-term results. But knowledge-based industries depend on investment in new products for long-term success. It is this transition failure that will have enormous cost implications. It will only be by getting to grips with the role change necessitated by waning power, that executives will avoid such a huge waste of potential.

Leaders with less power

What we are recognising through all the changes in organisational processes and ongoing shifts in power is that leadership is no longer exclusively associated with position. There are now knowledge leaders, people leaders, market leaders, innovation or product development leaders. Being a market leader is like leading in a golf tournament. If you are in the lead, you are in some sense ahead of your competition. Your goal is not to influence them to do anything, it is clearly just to stay ahead of them. You are a leader in such contexts by virtue of being ahead of others, not by virtue of your ability to persuade them to do anything. Your power is not the power to order people around, it is rather simply the power that propelled you into the lead in the first place. And this is the power to attract others to want to copy you so they can catch up and perhaps surpass you.

➡ **The essential point here is that organisational leadership is increasingly taking this form and divorcing itself totally from old-fashioned positional leadership.**

When we thought of leadership exclusively as the ability of someone in high office to command those lower down on the totem pole, our whole concept of leadership was completely internally focused. By contrast, a market leader is focused on his market not on his followers. Similarly, leaders in sporting events, like horse racing or golf, stay focused on their games if they are to stay in the lead, they do not think of their followers.

The theme of this discussion is that senior executives can still be leaders despite losing a lot of direct control over subordinates. They can lead in both process and content terms. If they are sufficiently entrepreneurial or 'opportunistic', they will sniff out opportunities and persuade others to join in pursuing them. Their goal ought to be *market leadership*. If you can be successful in achieving that, others will follow you automatically, so it is not a case of employing either formal or informal authority – the only choices available to you in old-fashioned leadership theory.

Inspiration must replace command.

Leadership from a process point of view is just being a catalyst for diverse groups of stakeholders, the ability to sense how to motivate and inspire people whose power is equal to, or greater than, your own.

The executive of tomorrow needs to be 'visioning', not necessarily to have a set, concrete vision, but to be able to inspire others to strive for larger possibilities. Inspiration must replace command. Today's leaders who have already made the transition to dealing with powerful customers and other stakeholders, will be best placed to develop new approaches to leading tomorrow's powerful knowledge workers.

FUTURE ROLES FOR SENIOR MANAGERS

Before the days of intense competition, no one had much choice, neither consumers nor employees. Business was much more monopolistic and complacent. At this time, we used to try to define management in monopolistic terms, that is one concept of management and leadership to fit all industries and all people. Situational leadership theory was the first dim recognition that there were a few shades of grey in the concept of leadership. Now, we can safely say that there never will be a universally applicable theory of leadership. The good news here is that it is up to entrepreneurially-minded managers to create their own conception of their roles as they study the needs of their own markets.

What is universally true, however, is that all managers will have to learn to live with less power and status as the business world becomes more democratic. All businesses will move, in organisational terms, towards the model on which hospitals, for example, or law firms are structured. In these industries, it is the professionals, the knowledge workers, who have the most power and status. Managers are often given a less lofty title in such environments: they are called administrators. So, management will become more of a service profession and less of a commanding/directing one as it was in the old military model.

➲ **The key to adapting to these imminent but profound changes is to find new sources of self-esteem and identity by leading the way in the search for new roles in your own markets.**

Just as many managers have found great satisfaction in serving customers better, they may repeat this successful transformation and find the same sense of achievement in fostering the growth of knowledge workers and inspiring greater team work among them.

PRACTICAL STEPS

➡ Take stock of the ways you have lost power to others already.

➡ Recognise that your desire for control is anxiety-driven, not rational.

➡ Work at scaling down your anxiety.

➡ Avoid the false sense of security associated with focusing only on short-term cost saving and productivity enhancement measures if you are in a knowledge-based industry.

➡ Think through what you have done to manage successfully anyway.

➡ Differentiate the ways in which you behave like a coach from the ways in which you are still trying to be a player.

➡ Devise new ways of influencing those with growing power.

➡ Define for yourself how you can show leadership.

➡ See how you can demonstrate 'market focused' leadership instead of being too preoccupied with downwards, internal leadership – think of leadership as being the first to get somewhere, like the leader in a golf tournament.

➡ Create a new role for yourself in which you can add even more value.

➡ Develop new meanings for the concepts of leadership and management.

SUMMARY

One of the most profound changes on the horizon that all managers will struggle to adapt to is the loss of power to a whole host of other stakeholders. Customers have already become kings, employees will be next. This will be the hardest shift to swallow. Still, there are all sorts of practical steps managers can take, both to view their roles differently and to create new roles for themselves. More subtle forms of power can take the place of the dictator's type of power. Influencing stakeholders more powerful than yourself is, after all, much, much more satisfying than trampling on the powerless.

In Chapter 9, we look at one more major personal transition; letting go at all career stages. We begin with letting go at retirement but apply underlying themes to transitions at all career stages.

'It is all that the young can do for the old,
to shock them and keep them up to date.'

George Bernhard Shaw, *Fanny's First Play*

LETTING GO –
THE ULTIMATE
CHALLENGE

OBJECTIVES

- To get to grips with letting go in all personal transitions, especially to younger employees.
- To learn to let go gracefully while always searching for new opportunities.

INTRODUCTION

In Chapter 7, we discussed one of the most difficult of all role changes to handle effectively, the transition from one organisation to a bigger job in a different organisation. The idea there was to try to shed light on all role changes by studying an especially difficult one. The same principle applies to this chapter. Letting go is a necessary skill for coping with all forms of personal change. By analysing why the most difficult form of letting go is so hard, we may be alerted to how we can all let go more gracefully no matter what changes we have to face.

EXAMPLE

He was Chief Executive of a large company he regarded as his own. He had founded the firm 35 years ago and, even though he was now only a 25 per cent shareholder, he still regarded it as *his* company. Now at 75 years of age, he seemed to be slowing down and the company's fortunes were also sagging.

Pressure from other stakeholders succeeded, after a protracted battle, in pushing him out the door, but he went kicking and screaming, not a bit gracefully. Why is it that so many senior executives hang on seemingly forever, well past their sell by dates? Why do some such executives bite your head off if you even hint at the question of when they plan to retire? Further, what does this have to do with coping with change more generally?

RETIREMENT – LETTING GO AT THE END

While we will be looking at why it is so difficult for older executives to retire in this chapter, the point is not so much to better understand retirement, but to get a better grip on all personal transitions of any magnitude. Retirement will thus only be used as the major example, along with others, of situations where letting go is painful but necessary to manage personal change successfully.

Never wanting to say goodbye

In his excellent book, *The Hero's Farewell* (1988, Oxford University Press, Inc.), Jeffrey Sonnenfeld analyses in depth the problems senior executives face at retirement age. Our discussion owes much to his thorough treatment. According to Sonnenfeld, some executives do manage to depart gracefully. It all seems to boil down to two main factors:

- how much of yourself you have invested in your role
- the extent to which you see yourself as having attractive options.

The idea here is that if your job is everything to you and you can see nothing else to do with yourself, the gap between now and after the transition seems like an unbridgeable chasm. We all need something to do in order to feel the sense of purpose on which our self-esteem depends.

Often, as Sonnenfeld found, a senior executive's departure is voluntary, albeit reluctant, and this will become more the norm as mandatory retirement gives way to cries of age discrimination. Where executives have some choice, they can be especially hard to get rid of. They manage to stay on as consultants in some cases, but this is often an excuse for continuing to rule from behind the scenes. Or they get themselves 'promoted' to Chairman of the Board but never let their replacement as Chief Executive manage without constant interference. Some even conspire to so undermine their successor that he fails, creating an excuse for the 'retired' Chief Executive to mount a rescue mission, proving once and for all that he is indispensable.

It is also not uncommon for a Chief Executive to make sure he hires subordinates who will never be up to filling his shoes. The strategy throughout his latter years seems to disempower possible successors so everyone will regard him as irreplaceable.

What we want to find out in this chapter is, first, why senior executives behave in this way and, second, what other examples are there of failure to let go in various organisational contexts. More importantly, what can you do to avoid the traps that could prevent you from letting go when you should?

Letting go as falling off a cliff

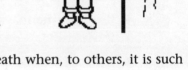

If you see yourself as having nowhere safe to fall, letting go becomes next to impossible, like falling off a cliff. Instead of letting go, you cling on for dear life.

Is retirement perceived as if it amounted to falling off a cliff? Reluctant retirees certainly cling to their roles with comparable tenacity. The question is why do they seemingly equate retirement with death when, to others, it is such a desirable transition?

We have alluded to at least a partial answer above. If the gap between how you see yourself now and how you see your alternatives is too great, then this gap is comparable to the height of the cliff you see yourself falling over. The greater the gap the more tightly you hold onto where you are. As with the distance between the top and bottom of a steep cliff, there are two factors which make the distance formidable: the position of the base of the cliff and the position of the top.

In the case of the reluctant retiree, the top of the cliff corresponds to how much he has invested in the status quo, while the bottom of the cliff equates to how much he feels that he would have to give up of what is important to him in order to make the transition to retirement.

What you have to give up to let go

This is difficult to specify in absolute terms, that is, distinct from what alternatives you might have to retire to. It's like trying to talk about the height of a cliff without talking about the distance between the top and the bottom! For example, one thing a senior executive might be loath to give up is the sense of importance he has acquired as reflected in the daily deference of others. But this is only a strong factor if you had no possibility of receiving similar deference after retirement, say as a consultant or part-time business school lecturer. If you had such a role to go to, then the gap would not be so great between today and tomorrow. So, it is not just a matter of what you are losing, in isolation. It clearly is the *relative* loss involved in the gap between what you have now and what you could have later.

Setting aside relativities for the moment, let's generate a list of possible things a prospective retiree might hate to lose:

- status, a feeling of importance, high regard paid by others
- the power to influence momentous events
- the feeling of still being alive, of still being able to contribute
- the excitement associated with winning in the heat of the battle
- working closely with admired and liked colleagues
- the opportunity to meet and rub shoulders with other powerful people
- being sought after for advice and being listened to avidly
- the need to feel you are earning a substantial living.

If you felt you could do some of these things on a smaller scale, say for a charitable organisation, perhaps the gap would not seem so formidable. But what could you envisage yourself going to, or losing, if you can see only a yawning chasm, with nothing at all attractive to go to? Possibly all or some of the following:

- the loss of all of the above good things
- boredom, inactivity, nothing to do but wait for death
- having to spend more time with a family you don't know very well

- loss of self-esteem and purpose in life
- fear of the unknown
- fear of having to face your own anxieties.

Dying to let go – letting go without dying

Without doubt, reluctant retirees fear that they are getting old and closer to death. Very likely, the single most important reason they cling onto their roles so tenaciously is that, compared to their more easy-going colleagues, they have an excessive fear of growing old and dying. All of the losses listed above really come down to the same thing: fear of death. Not many senior executives would admit to such a fear and it may not be conscious at all. But this is why they are tense, irritable and driven to prove to themselves and others that they are not over the hill yet.

It is not only senior executives who vainly struggle to cling to youthfulness, we see evidence all around us of similar yearnings. It is so common, for example, for wealthier old men to marry young women and generally to try to fool themselves into thinking that they are still young. Their efforts at self-deception will take the form of all sorts of immature behaviours that are more likely to fool themselves than anyone else. Hence, we see senior citizens over-exerting themselves in sporting activities, for example, so they can pretend to be still young.

In a senior executive, this struggle to seem younger could take the form of a puffed up sense of self-importance. It might manifest itself in expecting undue deference from 'inferiors' or being unnecessarily harsh in criticising their mistakes. The reason for the harshness is to prove that *he* would never make such a mistake, that *he* is still on top of things. Often, senior executives may be poor delegators because they need to prove that they are still able to do battle on the front line just as effectively as their juniors.

Even when people recognise, intellectually, that the end must come for us all at some point, they still may cling to past glories emotionally. So, intellectual recognition alone is no remedy for the tendency to keep striving to reclaim lost youth. An example of this is perhaps the famous golfer, Severiano Ballesteros who was quoted in *The Times* of London on 17 July 1996, commenting on his fading talents:

> 'I am proud to see what I did before. I am sad that I can't be youthful for ever, but nobody can do that. Everybody is going to die. That is the only truth in life, so you can't do anything about it.'

But this intellectual acceptance won't necessarily stop people from trying to stay young forever. We keep trying to make ourselves believe that we have lots of time yet.

As Jeffrey Sonnenfeld noted in his book, *The Hero's Farewell*, we admire heroes in sports, films and in the military because we want to be heroes ourselves. If you don't see yourself as terribly heroic in your job, you may find it easier to let go. But, chances are, the more you fancy yourself a hero, the more you hope you can keep it up. Like power, hero status is psychologically corrupting, making us addicted to a degree of adulation we would rather die than lose. The downside of striving to become a hero as a senior manager is that you create a seemingly unbridgeable gap between where you are and anywhere else.

> *Like power, hero status is psychologically corrupting, making us addicted to a degree of adulation we would rather die than lose.*

Letting go gracefully

As with jumping off a cliff, the key to retiring gracefully is to reduce the gap between where you are now and where you will be after retirement.

Part of the solution to reducing this gap is to recognise that it is entirely in your own mind. The gap you perceive between where you are now and where you should be is created by your own anxiety and fear of the unknown. But an essential step to take in order to fully appreciate that the gap is not so frightening after all is to start visiting your destination before making a wholesale, irrevocable move.

Just as the media sensationalises the crime rate in a country we might otherwise like to visit, but now are afraid to, our mind sensationalises the downside of situations that feel vaguely

Putting off facing a transition by building a bomb shelter around yourself will only make the inevitable seem that much more catastrophic when it finally happens.

unattractive. The result is that we create an image in our own minds of a horrible destination. Similarly, if you have an over blown self-image as an indispensable hero, you will have a lot of winding down to do in order to back away from such a high investment in your role. This is all the more reason to have worthwhile options in which to channel your self-esteem.

Applying these ideas to our reticent retiree, the best advice for him is to start building a new life away from the office, a retirement career in effect, before the time to depart actually arrives. As you develop other interests and get fully involved in them, the gap between where you are now and where you will be after retirement will not seem so awful. Instead, many senior executives go in the opposite direction. They so cling to the past that they cannot even contemplate retiring let alone beginning to explore retirement career options for themselves. This is clearly living in a fantasy world. Putting off facing a transition by building a bomb shelter around yourself will only make the inevitable seem that much more catastrophic when it finally happens.

As you develop your post-retirement career options, your anxiety will subside and you can begin to let up on yourself at work. This means handing over more to others, grooming successors and generally being more of a mentor to junior colleagues and less of a competitor in youth-orientated front line battles.

We noted in Chapter 1 that having some occupation that gives us a sense of accomplishment is essential for our self-esteem. This is just as true when you 'retire' as at any stage in your career. It does not matter what that occupation is as long as it is sufficiently interesting to give you a sense of self-worth.

LETTING GO AT ALL CAREER STAGES

We have discussed the hardest time to let go. While the key is surely to start developing other interests early so your departure is not so all-or-nothing, this is not to suggest that such a major transition is emotionally easy. Somehow you have to combine reconciling yourself to the inevitable with developing other interests so that you will create a softer landing for yourself.

Suppose now we move backwards in time a bit to consider what is involved in letting go at earlier stages in your career. We suggested earlier that if life could be considered a journey, it was probably best thought of as an uphill one until sometime around the age of 40 and downhill after that.

This view of your career journey implies that you should begin to think about various ways of letting go from about the age of 40. Obviously, this will vary from person to person, so long as this obvious fact is not used as an excuse to postpone any sort of letting go until you are approaching 60!

So, what are some of the things you need to start letting go of in mid-career? They might include:

- keeping up with your technical function to the same intense extent
- being an expert, content-orientated contributor, instead of leading
- needing to prove yourself largely through hands-on achievements
- competing so aggressively with younger colleagues
- the need to beat others at all costs, to never lose
- the continual impatience that makes you overly irritable
- your feeling of invincibility.

The most interesting question about this list is: What do all these issues have in common? First of all, they are all anxiety driven, but more importantly, as in our reluctant retiree's case, they all revolve around the fear of losing one's grip, of losing ground, especially to younger people.

➲ **The fear of decline and death is the fundamental basis of all resistance to change.**

Whatever our position on any issue and regardless of our career stage, any forced change will feel like a mini-death because it entails losing ground and letting go. At early career stages, letting go does not mean being over the hill or going out to pasture. It means regularly reviewing where you are in your journey and making occasional adjustments to your picture of yourself.

New role first, let go second

In Chapter 4, we looked at Tony, the 45-year-old engineering manager, and his struggle to redefine his identity. He wanted to hold onto his status as technical guru but he could see that he was losing ground to younger colleagues and he was under pressure to adopt a more fully managerial perspective. Until he could satisfy himself that he could find a new identity, a role he felt comfortable with, he was not able to let go of his old identity as the smartest technical expert in his department. The essence of letting go is always, as in the case of a senior executive's resistance to retirement, to find a new role first before you entirely let go of the past.

But, you might rightly object, don't you have to let go somewhat first to at least recognise that you should be letting go and hence that you should start looking for a new role? And isn't this initial recognition really the hardest part? After all, how can you begin thinking of new roles when you don't even see the need to let go in the first place?

Yes, this is a good point. If, like our reticent retiree, you reach the stage of vociferous denial and you have built a bomb shelter around yourself, chances are it will take a bomb to get through to you, to make you see what a fool you are making of yourself. Clearly, who would act so childishly if they recognised how they were behaving? And if you can't see how your resistance is causing you to be so irrational, how can you begin to look for alternative roles? The short answer is that once you reach this stage, you probably can't. It's most likely too late for managers once they are this locked into the status quo, unless they are somehow shocked into a greater self-awareness.

➲ **The better plan is to have options all the time so you don't wait until your anxiety is so high that your defences turn into an impenetrable bomb shelter.**

If you recognise ahead of time that you are going to experience an all too predictable need to hang onto your youth as you age, then, maybe, you will have some chance of adjusting to your steady decline gracefully. This is not to say that managers who do fade away gracefully, do so because of an explicit plan. No, it is more likely that they are just more laid back generally and/or have a wider range of interests in the first place, hence a broader perspective and a less narrow identity.

Most managers are likely to be somewhere in between these two extremes. They will neither have an explicit *letting go plan* from, say, the age of 30, nor will they become so unreachably locked into defensiveness that they will not recognise the need to change. For most of us, letting go will still be a struggle, but we will see the need in ourselves, if a bit belatedly at times. Regular feedback from others through 360-degree feedback will help us to keep in touch with reality.

EXAMPLE

To take Tony's case again. He realised that he was irrationally hanging onto his identity as a technical guru too long. He knew he would have to modify his identity somewhat, but he did not know how much or when or, indeed, in what specific direction. His dim awareness that something was wrong, because of his anxiety to stay ahead, was enough to start him groping for new roles. At this stage, he was still not totally convinced he had to change. But, he started by simply spending more time coaching and developing younger colleagues to see if he might find himself liking it. As he did, in time, grow to enjoy the management side more, then, and only then, was he able to begin to let go of some of his obsessive drive to keep up with so many areas of his technical field.

➲ So, again, the key point is to apply an experimental decision-making approach, to let yourself try options before making a decision.

It is a fundamental mistake to assume that we can make major personal decisions solely on the basis of navel gazing or introspection. It is only through direct experience of alternatives that we can make an informed choice among them. (For more on experimental decision making, see Chapter 3.)

THE ONSLAUGHT OF YOUTH

Giving way to younger people – are you up to it?

Younger people can all tell stories about even slightly older managers who seem to need to put younger employees in their place. Such stories all take the same form: younger employee makes a suggestion to his slightly older boss, only to be told how stupid the idea is and why it won't work. The tone of voice is nearly always somewhat condescending or patronising, only the excuses vary for rejecting the suggestion. If the rejection is not accompanied by a sneer it is with biting sarcasm, which is perhaps even more wounding.

The important point here is that the boss in such cases need not be over the hill, or even over 40. He or she could be 30, putting down a 25-year-old who just joined the organisation. Even at age 30, we have been around long enough to resent anyone younger appearing to know more about anything than we do. It makes us feel that we have missed something, that we have not progressed fast enough, if someone so much younger could already be ahead of us at such a young age. How irritating.

Letting go is, therefore, not only a pre-retirement issue. Letting go must start as soon as you find yourself working with any employees who are younger than you or newer to the organisation. If you do not make this conscious effort to let go, you will be resistant to change. Once you start holding on, you are starting to dig a dike around yourself for the sake of self-protection. The longer you do this the more you will need that dike and the deeper it will become. The message here is clearly to strive to avoid creating such defences in the first place.

Once you start holding on, you are starting to dig a dike around yourself for the sake of self-protection.

Why do we resent younger people so much? You don't, you say? Think again and you should be able to see it in yourself. If someone is promoted ahead of you, for example, is it not easier to accept if that person is older or the same age as you? What if he or she is five or ten years younger? How does that make you feel?

If the person is five or ten years younger, most managers will feel that they must really have wasted that much time. If you have not acquired enough valuable experience and skill to beat a person five or ten years your junior, who can you ever compete successfully against in your own age group?

Even if you admit to resenting the success of younger colleagues, just a tiny bit and only once in awhile, you may still object that this is not an emotion you can or need to change. Are you content to be labelled as resistant to change, then? If not now, then at some point in your career? The fact of the matter is that a lot of ideas for change will come from younger employees. Even if it is not a matter of fresh ideas, they are out to replace you simply by virtue of being lower in the organisational pecking order than you are at the moment. You do have a choice, however. You can resist the inevitable or recognise that, being only human, you will compete more aggressively with younger people simply because you see them as having no *right* to get ahead of you.

➲ **Constructive defensiveness here is to realise that we all feel the same way about this issue, so it is not a matter of your being uniquely pigheaded.**

Letting go to youth without being walked all over

You are likely to lose ground faster if you disdain all contact with younger colleagues as not worthy of your valuable time and attention. Conversely, if you recognise your resistance and accept the unavoidability of losing ground to youth, you can slow the process by picking up on their ideas faster, by orchestrating their imaginations so that you shine in their light.

 ➡ **The first step is to fully recognise this form of refusal to let go in yourself. Think of all the times you have told younger employees why some idea they suggested will not work. What did you feel at the time? Annoyance at their presumptuousness? To what extent were your objections rationalisations? No doubt some of their suggestions actually were impractical. Perhaps you felt particular glee at such times as you pointed out their errors. If you can honestly admit to such feelings, then you too have an**

issue with letting go, but your self-awareness is a vital first step to minimising its worst effects on you.

➡ The next step is to work at scaling down your emotional reaction. Some constructive self-defence is useful here. Tell yourself that this is inevitable for all people. You can't know everything anyway. Just because someone else has an idea you did not think of doesn't mean that you cannot make your own equally valuable contributions. Recognise that newer or younger people aren't necessarily smarter than you, they are just more naive. This naivety allows them to see things that you have become blind to because of over-familiarity. Children ask a lot of stupid questions, but some of their questions make us think about things we had taken for granted. Does this mean that your three-year-old child is smarter than you are? No, it simply means that his mental software has not yet been programmed to take certain things for granted, to process what is familiar to you automatically. You don't resent your child's silly questions because he is too young to compete against you for anything, unlike a slightly junior colleague.

➡ Next, start to think like an entrepreneur. When you recognise that the value added by youth comes from a fresh perspective and is no reflection on your abilities, start thinking of ways you can capitalise upon and develop this resource to benefit both you and your organisation.

Letting go in this context is not about finding a new role for yourself. It has to do with taking the pressure off yourself to stay forever young and with recognising the value you can add in your own right as a manager with a growing bank of experience.

So, letting go to youth does not mean laying down and dying. It means feeling proud of what you can contribute and taking advantage of the fresh perspective of younger people, looking for synergy with what you can offer.

➲ The key point is the realisation that you can't have it both ways. You can't have the wisdom and breadth of experience that comes with age and still maintain the freshness of youth. It is vital to see that the combination of your experience along with the fresh perspective of youth is an asset, not a loss.

This idea is easy to grasp intellectually, of course, but on the emotional side we all react to any hint of getting older no matter what benefits we might agree that age brings.

Sometimes an older manager might seem to excel in working closely with youth. It is important to be sufficiently 'self-critical' (see Chapter 6 for more on change competencies) to know whether you like to be around younger colleagues because you see their youth and your experience as complementary, or whether you are simply fooling yourself into thinking that you are still young in some sense yourself.

Letting go is partly about being more realistically competitive. A healthy level of competitiveness should not make you a poor loser, especially to younger colleagues. Even if one is promoted ahead of you, try to see rationally what this person had to offer for the role, but be sure to pat yourself on the back for what you have to offer as well.

Excessively-competitive managers either let themselves suffer too great a blow to their self-esteem when they lose or they harbour murderous resentment. When they win, highly-competitive managers gloat and abuse their success. Excessive competitiveness is self-defeating in the long term and in the broader picture because it will make you overly driven by destructive emotions that will inevitably reduce your receptivity to change.

Why is letting go so hard?

Throughout our lives we need to feel that we are making some sort of progress, neither stagnating nor, especially, slipping backwards. We seem to be most highly-motivated when we can see very visible signs that we are progressing along whatever dimension is important to us. Any sign that we are losing ground is like a sign of aging or of death – no matter how old or young we are.

Unfortunately, we tend to react most strongly to highly-visible signs. We are not particularly good at celebrating less tangible evidence of progress, like attaining a broader perspective or more wisdom. On the negative side, the more anxious we are about keeping up, the more sensitive we will be to the slightest signs of

> *When we can give ourselves full credit for whatever we have achieved, letting go of the need to win every issue will be far easier.*

losing ground. In this frame of mind, even imagined setbacks can be upsetting. When a younger colleague comes up with an idea we feel we should have thought of, what could be more visible? Immediately, we forget about all the value we have added recently in less visible ways and feel devastated by this more visible reminder of losing touch.

The implication of this discussion is that we should beware of the immediate and visible and learn to take better stock of the less visible ways in which we are making progress, becoming more mature, wiser, and more relaxed about some issues. When we can give ourselves full credit for whatever we have achieved, letting go of the need to win every issue will be far easier.

PRACTICAL STEPS

➡ Begin by recognising that not letting go is a major obstacle to change.

➡ Acknowledge that everyone has varying degrees of difficulty letting go.

➡ Face your own resentment of younger employees and fear of ageing.

➡ Monitor your desire to be a hero ensuring that you keep it in perspective.

➡ Recognise that new ideas do not negate the value of your contribution.

➡ Monitor and check your own tendency to put younger colleagues down.

➡ Stop feeling like a loser when others succeed; pat yourself on the back.

➡ Regularly review the less obvious ways in which you are progressing.

➡ Behave more entrepreneurially towards young colleagues.

➡ Where letting go requires a role change, try out the new before letting go.

➡ Most importantly, always view letting go as providing new opportunities.

SUMMARY

Letting go is an essential component of all major personal
transitions. It is not necessarily, contrary to the myth of
human rationality, the first step in a transition. You can let go
after experimenting with options. Having a range of options
and perspectives at your ready disposal at all times makes it
easier to let go of any one of them as needed. Seeing change in
entrepreneurial terms in this context means seeing letting go
as a process of generating fresh opportunities. If you see letting
go as dying, or anything equally horrible, this is your own
choice. It is not simply being realistic, being willing to face
reality. It is, rather, a chosen way of viewing yourself since you
can just as readily choose to look at letting go from an
entrepreneurial perspective. This approach is simply the
decision to view all change as providing you with fresh
opportunities. As long as you are aware of making this
choice, it can be a healthy way of operating rather than
defensive escapism.

Chapter 10 deals with the nebulous fears that managers have
of falling behind. It discusses how to cultivate a realistic
perspective to keep up as well as anyone can while
avoiding panic.

'Every man, wherever he goes, is encompassed by a cloud of comforting convictions, which move with him like flies on a summer day.'

Bertrand Russell, *Skeptical Essays*

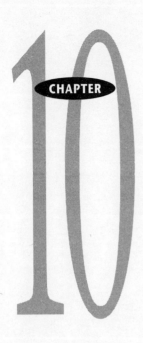

CHAPTER

WHEN TO CHANGE, WHEN TO LET GO

OBJECTIVES

- To set out some practical steps for coping with all the unexpected changes that will hit us in the future.

- To develop a balance of preparedness and realism in dealing with change.

INTRODUCTION

How do you know if you are resisting change or not? How do you decide what to keep up with and what to abandon? In the age of the information explosion, how can you keep up with anything?

KEEPING UP WITH TOMORROW

Managers are rightly worried about how they will keep up as the new millennium dawns and as the pace of change continues to accelerate. The first step, noted earlier, is to face the fact that no one individual will be able to keep up with everything. Businesses can diversify by having numerous separate divisions doing different things, but there is a limit to how much any one person can diversify. How many balls can you juggle at once?

As business grows more complex, we will inevitably, as individuals, have to specialise even more. This means more eggs in more limited baskets, at least as far as technical or functional job content is concerned. The danger of going the other way and becoming too general, however, is to totally lose touch with enough detail of any one field to add any value. You may be able to avoid over-specialisation, but if you are planning to opt for some sort of higher level liaison or intermediary role, you will still need to know enough about a few technical fields to understand the language of specialists and to sound credible yourself. In any case, the key is to think strategically about what you can usefully keep up with and to let go of what you can't.

Part of the reason managers fear slipping behind is that their fear is of something too nebulous. It is not the fear of something quite specific like missing that urgent deadline tomorrow. We can do something to overcome our fear of something specific. When we fear something more nebulous, however, we don't know what to do about it. This feeling of impotence, of course, only increases our anxiety. Mostly, the fear that managers feel towards the future is this nebulousness and uncertainty, it is less often something tangible.

The other reality we must face, along with not being able to keep up with everything, is that no one can predict the future. What this means is that no one will be any better off than we will. The good news is that the faster things change and the more complex the world becomes the more opportunities there will be for the entrepreneurially minded.

Keeping up with some things must be accompanied by letting go of others. If you think of yourself as a business, an entrepreneurial one at that, then you should think strategically, along with being 'opportunistic' (see Chapter 6) and prepared to 'improvise' in the face of the unexpected. Being strategic is part of 'visioning'. It means ensuring that you regularly review how you are spending your time and what new knowledge/skills you are acquiring. While you cannot predict the future, being 'market focused' will help you to make reasonable guesses about the way things are moving that will be as good as anyone else's best guesses. 'Networking' will help you to benchmark your guesses against those of a good circle of other people. The main point here is that by analysing what you are good at and what you want to carry forward, you are making the nebulous more specific and that automatically makes it more manageable.

> *The faster things change and the more complex the world becomes the more opportunities there will be for the entrepreneurially minded.*

If you do indeed take time to do periodic strategic reviews of where you are going, it is also essential to drop some things, keeping in mind that no business can be in everything. This is the harder part, though. This is where letting go comes into play. Here is a list of suggested strategic questions to ask yourself.

➡ **What am I doing that I could do in my sleep? Do I need to keep it up?**

➡ **What am I doing that I have been doing the same way for five years?**

➡ **What am I doing that I should be getting others to do?**

➡ **How much of my time is spent using knowledge recently acquired?**

➡ How much of what I am doing adds no great value in my market?

➡ What have I stopped doing or passed onto others recently?

No doubt you can think of some better strategic questions to ask yourself and certainly many more. The point is that you should make time to do this strategic review in your own terms if you are sincere about continually renewing yourself to deal effectively with change as opposed to drifting into the future.

The next step is to accept that this is as good as anyone can do, so it is important that you put your anxiety in its place and not let it rule your life.

How can you tell if you are resisting change?

Resistance to change has the advantage over the fear of falling behind that it is at least not nebulous. If you are resisting change, try to identify if it is something quite specific you are resisting. It may help to keep a little check-list handy of possible irrational reasons why you are objecting to someone else's idea. If you can go through this list and honestly conclude that none of them applies to you, then perhaps your objections are reasonably rational and not symptoms of resistance to change. Such a check-list might include such questions as the following.

➡ Do I object to the person proposing the change?

➡ Do I resent not having been involved at an earlier stage?

➡ Do I have something to lose by this change?

➡ Do I resent the manner in which this change has been proposed?

➡ Am I angry that I did not come up with this idea myself?

➡ Do I fear/dislike having to give up a favoured way of doing things?

If you find yourself answering 'yes' to any of these questions, your objections to the change may be less rational than you think. You may still find this hard to accept because some of your objections may be perfectly sensible, such as, your criticism of the cost or the timing of the change.

⮑ The problem here is that you may be hiding your irrational objections behind quite sensible ones, thereby fooling yourself into thinking that you are being totally reasonable.

If you have answered 'yes' to any of the questions on this check-list, you should be 'self-critical' (remember the change master competencies in Chapter 6) and try to analyse as objectively as you can why it is that you have answered 'yes' to one of the questions.

To get yourself out of this counterproductively defensive mode, you should try to generate a list of all the good reasons to back the proposed change. You should do this on paper as this will make the case appear to you to be more convincing. You should also ask others to add to your list to ensure that it is comprehensive. This may seem like a contrived exercise, but experiments have shown that writing essays extolling the virtues of, say, the police, has helped to change the attitudes of those writing them, i.e. the people who had negative attitudes towards the police in the first place. This was shown by having such people do attitude surveys regarding the police before and after writing their essays praising them.

If you can now admit to objecting to the change on less than rational grounds and you are beginning to see some merit in the idea, the next step is to be 'selfless' and talk yourself into putting the organisation's welfare first. Finally, be 'opportunistic' and get on the bandwagon yourself.

How do you know if you are keeping up?

Here it is a matter of doing your own feedback surveys, canvassing the attitudes of colleagues and internal or external customers who know you well enough to comment. You should pick people to give you feedback who you regard as keeping up-to-date. It would be a good idea to include some of your younger colleagues as well. To obtain useful feedback, it is important to ensure that you ask meaningful, tough questions. This means asking questions that are focused on those areas where keeping up is important to you, but also more general questions so that people giving you feedback can put their finger on other topics as well.

You might begin your questionnaire by stressing how important honest feedback is to you. Then you might say that you have been trying to keep up to date in X, Y and Z fields. You should then say something like: 'Please rate me on a one to six scale in terms of how you think I am doing.' Next you might ask a question like: 'In what ways do you see me as falling behind the times?' and 'What suggestions can you offer to help me keep up?'

Through a combination of regular feedback (probably obtained anonymously), staying 'market focused' and benchmarking yourself through 'networking', you will do as much as anyone can do to ensure that you are keeping up with whatever is important to you.

> *To obtain useful feedback, it is important to ensure that you ask meaningful, tough questions.*

How do you know when to let go?

You never will know precisely when is the right time, but you should be letting go of something all the time, given today's rate of change. The best you can do is take a number of steps to ensure that you are regularly letting go of your fair portion of bad habits, obsolete skills and outdated attitudes. Below are some suggested steps:

➡ **Make sure that you diversify yourself as much as you can.**

➡ **Acquire new skills and change roles regularly.**

➡ **Make sure you drop familiar, routine activities regularly.**

➡ **Go out of your way to encourage young people, watching yourself to ensure that you are not resenting their progress.**

➡ **Develop outside hobbies or occupations that will make retirement an attractive proposition for you when the time comes.**

➡ **Ask yourself why you want to hang onto some activities and ensure they fit with your strategic aims if you do not want to give them up.**

HELPING OTHERS CHANGE

We have been focusing too one-sidedly on you and your feelings. We said a few times that activity and an external focus were good remedies for the stalemate resulting from too much inward focus on an organisational level and too much introspection on a personal level.

One good solution to this problem is to spend more time, as a mentor, helping others to change. If you can coach others through some of the fears and anxieties we have discussed here, you are more likely to forget your own and to see more clearly how much progress you have made yourself.

To help others, develop your coaching skills

The essence of good coaching is getting others to think for themselves and to solve their own problems. This means stifling your own temptation to give them your solutions. Active listening is the means of drawing others out effectively. This entails asking lots of questions – open questions that cannot be answered by 'yes' or 'no'. Finally, a good coach should gently help others construct a personal change plan, including the public commitment and feedback elements we discussed in Chapter 5.

USING A MENTOR YOURSELF

The best sports figures in any sport use personal coaches to help them improve so they can live up to their full potential. Why do managers feel they do not need a coach? It is odd that they feel this way in view of the fact that so many of them complain of having no one to talk openly to. Perhaps this is one change that too many managers are resisting. Resistance to change certainly has a lot to do with feeling that you must be strong enough to carry everything on your own shoulders. If you can set aside this old-fashioned attitude, maybe you will be more receptive to having a coach

Resistance to change certainly has a lot to do with feeling that you must be strong enough to carry everything on your own shoulders.

or mentor to serve as a sounding board and to help you with your change issues. A good mentor can be a senior executive, someone recently retired, a trusted human resources professional or an external consultant. The key is to pick someone you respect and feel comfortable communicating with openly.

How much do I have to change and what if I don't want to?

As you age, you may increasingly wonder whether the pace of change you are having to maintain is worthwhile. The bottom line has to do with your personal values. No one can drive you to keep up but yourself. The only important consideration is that you make a conscious choice either to stay in the race or drop out in accordance with your own values. Dropping out simply because you feel defeated is likely to leave you with bad feelings. This is why regular strategic reviews are a better idea than simply reacting to an immediate sense of exhaustion or resignation.

Dropping out is only likely to feel like the end for you if, as we have already seen, you have nothing to drop out to. This is why it is critical to maintain a few viable options at all times for alternative occupation and self-worth.

If you are in a knowledge-driven industry, keeping up with new ideas will be more important and harder than in slower-changing, more mature or more labour-intensive industries. Because we will need to think of alternative occupations or careers as medical science enables us to live longer, it is important to be continually cultivating some fall-back options. One course of action may be to move from a fast-changing, highly-competitive industry to one that is a little slower-paced. If you have maintained a number of leading-edge skills, then such a move should not be too difficult even in your fifties or sixties.

IN CONCLUSION

As the pace of change increases, we will all have to change faster and let go of more of the past faster. As we develop our personal change skills and strategies, this should not be as oppressive as it is today when many of us seem simply overwhelmed by change. Ironically, as change accelerates, there ought to be more roles for consolidators, people who can deliver today's business efficiently and keep things on the rails now while the rest of the world races ahead. There has to be an upper limit to how much change we can cope with, so there will always be some need for a balance between change and consolidation. In fact, as change becomes more chaotic, those able to consolidate may be in greater demand than those who can create the new.

The good news here is that this is another market for the skills of managers who would rather not drive themselves so relentlessly to keep up. Importantly, this then may be another avenue for letting go.

Worms into butterflies, frogs into princes – final comments on change

While we are advocating a form of ongoing self-renewal, let's acknowledge straightaway that none of us can be reborn or transform ourselves into butterflies. We can learn to see each stage of our lives and all changes as providing us with new opportunities. And we can strive to maintain a realistic perspective on ourselves, the world and our place in it, but we are not going to fundamentally alter our basic personalities or turn back the clock. Managing personal transitions effectively is more about understanding our emotional reactions to them and dealing with them as maturely as possible than it is about self-transformation. Learning to manage ourselves through change includes picking up some useful skills and techniques, but it is not a fountain of youth. Don't be deluded by hype, we are all in the same boat.

The essence of managing transitions well is to prepare for them by continually developing options and new perspectives while always working to see the unexpected as a fresh opportunity. This includes regularly patting yourself on the back for your achievements instead of dwelling on your losses.

PRACTICAL STEPS

➡ Accept that neither you nor anyone else can keep up with everything.

➡ Make nebulous fears concrete by looking at your assets strategically.

➡ Break down all you are doing and reject whatever does not fit your strategy – discard anything that smacks of the overly familiar, routine or obsolete.

➡ Network to benchmark how up-to-date you are relative to others.

➡ Accept that no one can predict the future, so we all have to live with a certain amount of anxiety regarding the unknown.

➡ Work at minimising your anxiety about the future by convincing yourself that more complexity and change mean more opportunities.

➡ Keep your nose to the ground and one eye on the bigger picture, i.e. be 'market focused' – this is as close as anyone can keep to the future.

➡ Create and use a check-list of possible irrational excuses you may be using to resist change – catch yourself at it and strive to take a more positive approach.

➡ Regularly review the change master competencies in Chapter 6 and continue to work at improving your performance against them.

➡ Get regular feedback on how you are doing with respect to your change efforts.

➡ Help others change to take your mind off yourself.

➡ Make use of a trusted coach or mentor.

➡ Work harder at relaxing.

SUMMARY

As long as you have options, letting go can be seen as a positive step rather than as losing or giving up. Strategically, it is vital to get clear about your own personal values and mission in life so that you know what new directions are best for you and when to pursue them rather than letting yourself get stuck in a no-win rut. If you become fed up with the pace of change, find yourself a slower-moving environment. It is up to you whether you see this as just good business sense or defeat. You can let go of quite a lot while still finding new opportunities to interest and stimulate you. It all depends on how you look at it. You can't control the inevitable, only how you view it.

MONTENEY
LEARNING
CENTRE

INDEX